OAT
CUISINE

QUAKER

Quaker Oats are pleased to bring you this special edition of OAT CUISINE. We hope you enjoy finding out the many different ways in which oats can add new dimensions to your cooking — whether in casseroles, soups, snacks, main courses, desserts or in baking. And, of course, perfect for porridge itself.

100% *PURE AND NATURAL*

Quaker Oats are rolled porridge oats, made only from the finest, selected oats. Once we've milled them, we do very little else. There are no additives or preservatives in our porridge oats. No other breakfast cereal is as *naturally* good for you.

THE BEST WAY TO START THE DAY

As porridge, Quaker Oats provide a filling, nutritious and warming breakfast, yet only amount to 113 Kcalories per bowlful, about the same as a bowl of cornflakes. Alternatively, how about starting the day with a super nutritious morning cocktail, delicious oat cakes or grilled grapefruit, and all made with Quaker Oats.

NO OTHER BREAKFAST CEREAL HAS A HIGHER LEVEL OF SOLUBLE FIBRE THAN OATS

Oats contain a special sort of fibre, *soluble fibre*. Clinical tests have shown that soluble fibre can have benefits in reducing blood sugar and cholesterol levels. All the delicious recipes in OAT CUISINE have been chosen with this in mind.

OAT
CUISINE

Pamela Westland

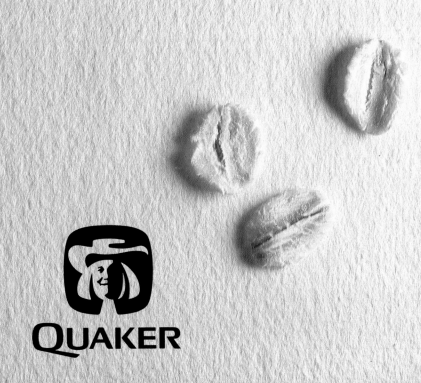

QUAKER

House editor Susan Dixon
Designed by Niki Penn
Line drawings by Judith Cheek
Text filmset in Novarese
by Dorchester Typesetting

Printed and bound in Spain by Cayfosa, Barcelona
Dep. Leg. B · 28808-1985

Contents

Notes

It is important to follow *either* the metric *or* the imperial measures when using the recipes in this book. Do *not* use a combination of measures.

All spoon measures are level.

All recipes serve four people unless otherwise specified.

Acknowledgements

Food photography   Grant Symon
Home Economist   Jane Suthering
Stylist   Penny Markham

Oats for photography provided by Quaker Oats Limited.

Introduction

What's in an oat? How much is packed into that insignificant-looking little grain? The answer, I suspect, is more than one would think.

First and foremost, there's survival on a great scale, for cereals alone still support and nourish half the world, and across several continents and over thousands of years oats have played their part. The seed has germinated and flourished in soils too poor, too wet and too cold to play host to other, less hardy grains. And so oats have reached parts of the world where, generations ago, other cereals could not reach.

Then there's nutritional value. A chapter a few pages further on outlines the way that modern medical research is pointing. To tell us something that Britons – yes, it has to be said, the Scots and the Welsh particularly – North Americans, Scandinavians and other Northern and Eastern Europeans seem always to have known: that oats are good for you. *How* good, is the subject of continuing and immensely rewarding research. To say that the soluble fibre content of oats has been found actually to be an effective treatment in severe cases of diabetes and high blood cholesterol is to put it in a nutshell. And to indicate that a daily intake of oats can be an effective preventive measure in these and other ailments.

And then there's flavour. No other cereal tastes like oats. There's that slightly sweet, slightly sour taste that I have likened to 'dry yoghurt'. There's a depth to the flavour that prevents it from being bland – and that should help to keep eager fingers away from the sugar bowl.

And there's adaptability. With fresh and dried fruits, in baked goods and desserts, oats seem the perfect 'sweet' accompaniment. With vegetables, cheese, fish and meat they seem the natural partner to savouries. And blended with other grains – with wholewheat flour in pastry and bread, for example, oats really prove that, in terms of flavour, they have the dominant genes. Moreover, they are in many ways interchangeable. You can, for example, equally well toss herrings in rolled oats or any grade of oatmeal, and fill them with a herby mixture based on cooked groats, oatmeal or rolled oats. To thicken sauce you can use fine or medium oatmeal, oat bran or oat flour, and in baking you can vary the texture according to whether you use oatmeal or rolled oats.

Lastly, but very closely linked with all the other factors, there's tradition. Whole nations have been programmed, deep within their cultures, to sit companionably around the breakfast table savouring the warmth and satisfaction of a bowl of steaming porridge. And now new generations, still faithful to the grain, are following the lead of the Swiss physician, Dr Bircher-Benner, and making that nutritious and companionable bowl one of muesli. The recipe that he devised early this century, it is worth recalling, was for rolled oats, raw apple, lemon juice, hazelnuts and milk. And that, he averred, constituted a perfectly balanced meal.

Since I began writing this book, people have said to me, 'But isn't it terribly dull? Doesn't the food all taste the same?' With chapters on breakfast dishes, snacks, soups and casseroles, main dishes, accompaniments, desserts and baking, I haven't found it the least bit dull to write.

As to all the food tasting the same, well there's a world of difference, it seems to me, between, for example, mushroom pâté and lemon soup; carrot crumble and leeks in white wine; spiced lentil pilaf and pheasant packed with herby oatmeal; summer pudding and banana tea bread; oat cakes and cheese and herb bread. But you must be the judge.

Full of Goodness

Oats have never suffered at the hands of the diet fads and fancies that have beset other foods; the swings and roundabouts of being recommended by an impressive string of experts one year, only to be declared completely taboo the next. No, oats have always enjoyed the reputation of being 'good for you', though it is only very recently that medical research has advanced to the point where this instinctive knowledge can be well substantiated.

One of the reasons for this health-image consistency is that oats, unlike wheat, have not fallen victim to food technology. They have not had the 'goodness' milled out of them and been offered for sale in a refined and abused state, as high-rise flour and light-as-air processed foods. Actually, they couldn't be, for oats are very low in gluten. This means that the flour milled from them will not rise in baking, with or without the bran. So almost certainly it is this natural deficiency which has saved them from the clutches of the food do-badders. They have had, perforce, to leave oats where they have always been – as groats, rolled, flaked, cut or ground, but nutritionally *complete*.

THE COMPOSITION OF THE GRAIN

When oats are harvested, the panicle, or frond, consists of stalks that hold the oat kernel inside the outer husk, or chaff. The whole oat remains when the chaff has been winnowed away. To the farmer this grain is the seed for the following year's crop. To the food manufacturer the whole oat is the raw material that forms the basis of all oat cereal products.

Each grain consists of an outer coating which comprises the bran, endosperm and germ, or embryo. In wheat, it is the bran and much of the germ that are processed out to leave an incomplete and nutritionally diminished product – white flour.

Whole oats contain (according to a standard work on the composition of foods*) 72.8 per cent carbohydrate, which is essential for body energy; 12.4 per cent protein, which is needed for growth; 8.7 per cent fat, balanced between polyunsaturated and saturated fatty acids, and significant amounts of potassium, magnesium, calcium and phosphorus.

Studying the vitamin content of oats gives a reassuring nutritional picture. Go to work on a bowl of oats and you provide your body with the get-up-and-go of vitamin B_1, *thiamine*, which serves to convert carbohydrates into energy in both muscles and nervous system; B_2, *riboflavin*, which, together with oxygen, is needed by the body to convert into energy amino acids from proteins, fatty acids from fats, and sugars from starches, to produce and repair body tissues and maintain healthy mucus surfaces; *niacin*, one of the vitamin B complex, which also helps to produce energy from carbohydrates, fats and proteins, and is essential for the correct functioning of the brain and nerves and the maintenance of healthy skin, tongue and digestive organs. Also present in that cereal bowl is vitamin B_6, *pyridoxine*, and vitamin E, *tocopherol*. What oats do not contain, however, is vitamin C, at least not until the germination process is begun and they are sprouted – see page 77 for the simple-as-child's-play instructions.

THE FIBRE STORY

So much for the nutritional element of the grain. But what of that non-nutritional yet vitally beneficial component so much in the news these days, the dietary fibre? It is in this area that much recent medical research has been concentrated, and which has produced some revealing and – medically speaking – exciting facts.

A team of researchers at Kentucky University in the United States, led by Dr James Anderson, has been isolating the different properties of the two distinct types of dietary fibre present in the cell walls of plants. One type, easily recognizable in the dry-as-dust form of wheat bran, for example, is termed water-insoluble. The other, known as soluble fibre, can be identified as the sticky, gummy substance in oats that makes a non-stick pan almost a 'must' when making porridge, and as the slippery, translucent substance that forms a protective coating around tomato seeds.

All plants contain some dietary fibre, and of both types, but it is found in greatly differing

McCance and Widdowson's The Composition of Foods. Fourth revised edition by A A Paul and D A T Southgate. Published by Her Majesty's Stationery Office.

proportions. Wheat and nuts have more insoluble than soluble fibre, while oats, barley and rye are good sources of the water-soluble type.

Lack of dietary fibre in the Western diet, due to the preponderence of refined and non-plant foods, has made our society prone to a long list of ailments, many of them killers. It is no coincidence that the illnesses are collectively referred to as 'Western diseases'. They include coronary heart disease, the commonest cause of death; cancer of the large bowel; appendicitis and diverticular disease of the colon – the most common disorders of the intestine; gallstones; obesity; diabetes; haemorrhoids; varicose veins and tooth decay. A formidable list indeed!

The properties of water-insoluble fibre such as wheat bran are well known after the welter of publicity given in recent years to high-fibre diets. This type of fibre acts as roughage, bulks up the waste materials in the body, and speeds their passage through the digestive system.

Soluble fibre, which swells as it absorbs water in the intestine, carries sugars further down the bowel before they are absorbed, and also, it seems, delays the process of emptying the stomach. This has the secondary effect of curbing the anticipation of the next snack or meal.

Slow-release foods

With the latest research findings, new phrases are creeping into our vocabulary. We learn that some foods high in fibre are termed 'slow-release foods', and that they are a good thing. It has been found that whole grains of all kinds – wheat grains, brown rice and others – products such as wholewheat semolina and pasta which are made from coarsely ground grains (as distinct from bread, which is made from finely ground flour), and soluble fibre all help other foods present in the intestine to release their energy components slowly. This is the very reverse, clearly, of sugar, which is a quick-release food and often deprecatingly dubbed empty calories.

Further, a decade of medical trials by Dr Anderson has produced evidence that *beta glucan*, the soluble fibre found in cereals, has helped to control and reduce harmful levels of sugar and cholesterol in the blood.

This has been of particular benefit to sufferers from diabetes, which is commonly caused by an excess of sugar in the blood, created by the body's inability to control the balance between its own sugar production and the sugars consumed. Dr Anderson's high carbohydrate/fibre diet, based on the soluble fibre in oats, has meant that many patients have been able to give up the standard insulin treatment entirely and others to reduce their intake considerably.

The same medical team has found that harmful cholesterol levels in men show a reduction of some 20 per cent after a diet supplemented by oat bran. Since it is the build-up of excess cholesterol which can lead to hardening and eventual blockage of the arteries and heart valves, the value of these findings cannot be over-estimated.

THE CALORIE COUNT

Many people who, without perhaps being able to quote chapter and verse, have never doubted the nutritional and other health advantages of oats, do, however, harbour suspicions on one point. The myth lingers still that oats, whether they are enjoyed raw as muesli, cooked as porridge or served in any other way, are fattening, which is, to put it mildly, unfair.

Assume that a 25g/1oz serving of oats or oatmeal contains about 95 Kcalories and you have to admit that whatever else it is in the cereal bowl that makes you fat, it isn't going to be the grain. Take a bowl of crunchy muesli or a steaming plate of porridge, however, and stir in generous amounts of nuts, dried fruits, full-fat milk or yoghurt and even the smallest amounts of sugar or honey, and you pile on the calories. But don't blame the oats!

It is not, however, only in terms of their own limited calorific value that oats can contribute to a slimming or weight maintenance programme. In common with all high-fibre foods, they have the effect of reducing hunger by invoking a feeling of fullness and meal satisfaction. That way they play an important part in the psychology of slimming, or what may be termed 'food intake control'.

In short, a bowl of oats for breakfast *instead* of a plate of sausages, egg and bacon, or a main course or dessert made with oats, instead of cholesterol rich or harmful sweet ingredients, will both avoid any temptation to embark on a calorific binge and, eaten regularly, will also provide the basis for a healthy diet, and moreover, one that is rich in flavour and texture.

Shopping Around

The increasing present-day popularity of oats must represent one of the most remarkable marketing phenomena of all time. It can't often come about that a product known to have been around for several thousand years suddenly attracts a massive surge of interest and enjoys a sales boom. It isn't, after all, these days, as if we are low on choice. There was a time when oats were the staple food of whole countries and parts of continents for no better reason than that they, above all other cereals, grew there most readily, in the prevailing climate and soil conditions. Not so now. With improved, more hardy strains of other cereals, and modern transport and communications systems, shops are packed with as wide a choice as one could wish for – ranging between brown rice, golden cornmeal, cracked wheat, rye flour, barley flakes and buckwheat to name just a few among them.

No, it must have something to do with the distinctive, slightly sweet, slightly sour flavour; quite a bit to do with the versatility in cooking of all kinds, and a great deal to do with their health-maintaining properties, that oats are experiencing such a thrust of product loyalty.

FROM FIELD TO TABLE

Six producing nations split up 75 per cent of the world's annual oat crop: the United States, USSR, Canada, Poland, Germany and France. The remainder is produced in the United Kingdom, Denmark, Sweden, Czechoslovakia, Australia and Argentine.

In some countries, the seed is usually sown in the spring and combine-harvested in August and September, weighing in at the mill with a moisture content of around 16 per cent. It is then cleaned and graded, then sifted and kiln-dried. In this, perhaps the most important of the processes, the grains are partially toasted by currents of hot air, to emerge with a moisture content reduced to 6-7 per cent, and with the sealed-in characteristic flavour and aroma of the oat.

After more cleaning and grading, the grains are hulled and then, in the age-old winnowing process, the tough, light outer husks are blown away. This at last reveals the oat groat, which is the whole grain, almost cylindrical in shape, blunt at the germ end and pointed at the 'beard' end.

From this point the groats are subject to different processes, depending upon the form in which they are destined to appear on the shop shelves.

Stabilization

If you have ever come across an oat product that smelled rancid or tasted bitter, then it probably had not undergone an extra heat or steam treatment. An enzyme present in the grain, *lipase*, converts the natural oil to glycerine and fatty acids which, though important to plant development, result in deterioration in flavour in the ungerminated grain. The heat treatment which is part of the rolling and flaking process – to manufacture porridge oats – kills this enzyme. Oatmeal of all grades, plus oatbran and oatgerm all need heat-stabilizing.

Types of oat products

The wholegrain oat is processed to produce several distinctly different though often interchangeable forms of oats.

When you are shopping, there is no substitute for reading the labels. Only then can you be sure you buy what you want to buy.

Oat groats

As mentioned earlier, these are the complete, wholegrain oats. They resemble long-grain brown rice to some extent in appearance and, indeed, in use, and are available mainly through health-food shops.

Jumbo oats

These round flat rolled oats, the largest of the oat products, are descriptively named. They are produced from the whole oat grain, steam-treated to stabilize and soften it, then lightly rolled. The oats are of uniform size, creamy white flecked with brown, and familiar as the firm, dry, crunchy ingredient in muesli.

Rolled porridge oats and oat flakes

Smaller than jumbo oats though otherwise similar in appearance, rolled porridge oats, also called oat flakes, are made from coarse, pinhead oatmeal. The oatmeal is first steamed to de-activate the enzymes, then passed through heavy rollers to crush and flatten it. The rolled oats are highly versatile and can be used in everything from crumble toppings to salad dressings, bread to baked vegetable fillings.

Oatmeal

There are three main grades of oatmeal – *pinhead*, which is the coarsest, followed by *medium* and *fine*. All are produced by cutting the oat groats.

Pinhead oatmeal – called short oats in the United States – looks like exactly what it is, the whole processed grain neatly chopped into three. It is best soaked overnight and then simmered in soups, casseroles, fruit dishes and, of course, porridge.

Medium and fine grades of oatmeal are made by further reducing the cut oats by means of rollers. They are excellent thickening agents and, unlike pinhead oatmeal, can be added to dry baked goods such as breads and pastry.

Oat flour

Not widely available, oat flour is cut to a very fine texture. It can easily be made at home by grinding jumbo oats, rolled oats or oatmeal in a blender or food processor. Alternatively, fine oatmeal can be substituted.

Oat bran

Produced with a high content of outer seed casing, or bran, of finely ground groats, it is the bran which contains the highest concentration of soluble fibre in the grain. It is available in health-food shops as an individual product, or packaged under a brand name as oatbran and oatgerm – the germ being the kernel of the grain. These products are stabilized for ensured quality, and can be added to bread, scone and pastry mixtures, fillings, toppings and muesli, in addition to being sprinkled over soups and desserts.

Packaged cereals

There are a number of ready-packaged breakfast cereals competing for the mighty porridge and 'instant hot cereals' space on the supermarket shelves.

Some are simply jumbo oats or rolled oats packaged with the manufacturer's quality guarantee. Some rolled oats have been partly pre-cooked to cut down on precious breakfast-time minutes; others, known as instant oats, consist of flakes mixed with oat flour. Yet others have added vitamins, iron, wheat bran, sugar or salt. The permutations are seemingly endless.

Varying your Oats

You could sit down at breakfast in Denmark to a plate of raw oatmeal sprinkled with milk and sugar – the forerunner of muesli?; move on to Finland for a taste of oat kissel, a creamy wholegrain dessert served with butter and herbs or spices; spoon up a dauntingly thick onion and oat soup in France; down a refreshing and restorative glass of oats and water in Africa; share a nutritionally boosted meat and oat casserole with a Muslim family preparing for Ramadan; and be approached on a visit to Pakistan, where the grain has a high currency value, by a black marketeer saying 'Psst! Want to buy a can of rolled oats?' For oats certainly get around the globe.

No-one knows when and where the first wild oats grew. Oats are known to have been under cultivation, in plants bred from the wild, in the Near East in 2500 BC, and traced on Iron Age sites in Asia. Virgil wasn't a member of the oats fan club – he 'had but little esteem' of them, but generally the Greeks and Romans recognized their nutritional and culinary value. And so oats, in company with so many plants, made the trek across Europe and went everywhere the Romans went. Which made sense, for the advancing armies colonized some places with pretty cool, wet climates, and their oats just thrived and thrived.

THE POPULARITY OF PORRIDGE

The Scots, who had firmly established oats alongside barley as a staple cereal crop by the 13th century, claim porridge as their own. There are other claimants too: the Vikings set great store by it; in Ireland, and Wales where it is called brewis, people have been going to work on it for hundreds of years; in Norway they serve it with soured cream; and in West Africa it carries the reputation of giving power and health to young and old. In the Northern United States, another region where the inclemency of the climate is an open invitation for oats to flourish, *their* porridge is made by combining pinhead oatmeal with water and eating it raw.

PORRIDGE PLUS

Purists may jib, but porridge doesn't *have* to be oatmeal or rolled oats simmered to a creamy consistency, and nothing else. A bowl of porridge has the potential for as many variations as a muesli mix. Whether you choose pinhead oatmeal, jumbo oats, rolled porridge oats or, indeed, a mixture, the flavouring variations are endless.

Try a sweet and sour dressing of lemon or orange juice and a drizzle of honey; a cored and chopped dessert apple tossed with ground ginger, cinnamon or grated nutmeg; sliced banana tossed in lemon juice and shredded coconut; a handful of dried fruit and nuts; a floaty layer of wafer-thin dried banana 'chips'; or, slightly more eccentric perhaps, 1 × 15ml spoon/1 tablespoon chopped parsley, marjoram, mint or thyme stirred into each portion of porridge.

Just as the Nigerians do, you can make a nutritious drink by stirring 1-2 × 15ml spoons/1-2 tablespoons of medium oatmeal or rolled porridge oats into a glass of iced water or chilled skimmed milk. Try further variations, using unsweetened fruit juice such as apple, pineapple, orange, blackcurrant or raspberry, and, if possible, including a slice or two of fruit. Stir oatmeal or rolled oats into a glass of chilled fruit purée, thinned down, if needed, with milk or buttermilk, and sprinkle a few toasted oats or nuts on top. Served with one or two oat cakes, it's a meal in itself.

Oats blended variously with grated cheese, low-calorie cottage cheese, chopped nuts and rubbed-in low-cholesterol margarine make deliciously golden savoury and sweet crumble toppings for vegetables, fish, meat and fruit dishes. The Romans gave us the idea – they had a delicious creamy chicken dish with an oaty crumble topping and dreamy oat-topped cheesecake. Scone dough with the pleasantly sour flavour of oats makes a hearty cobbler topping. And, with the low proportion of fat to flour, and no sugar, scones are among the healthiest baking you can find.

NOT-SO-LEAVENED BREAD
The poor raising properties of oats mean that baked goods have to compensate in terms of flavour for what they lack in lightness. The Welsh get round this problem by disguising the chewy toughness of Siot, an oat cake, by dipping it in buttermilk.

Oats give a deliciously 'different' flavour to breads if fine oatmeal or oat flour are blended with wholewheat flour in the proportion of, say, one to four for wheat bread with an oaty flavour, and in the proportion of one (oats) to two (wheat flour) for a flatter, heavier but deliciously oatier loaf; or if jumbo or rolled porridge oats are added to bread and scone doughs, and tea bread mixtures, thereby giving both crunch and bite.

For a powdery topping, a dusting of fine oatmeal is ideal on baked goods; and, moving up the scale, crunch can be provided by pinhead oatmeal, rolled oats and oat groats.

A HANDFUL OF OATS
Straight from the jar, a handful of oats is quicker than making breadcrumbs as the basis for fish, poultry and meat stuffings, or to coat whole fish or chicken and veal escalopes.

Cut down on saturated fat – housekeeping money too – by 'extending' minced meat in sauces for pasta, vegetable fillings – stuffed aubergines or peppers maybe – and meat loaves by stirring in oatmeal or rolled porridge oats. After all, that's what the Scots do in haggis, that controversial mixture of offal, oatmeal and lard, and skirlie, or mealie pudding, a type of white sausage.

Oats do a good job of soaking up fruit juice or thickening stewed fruit, and can be scattered over a pastry base to stop it becoming soggy.

Use oat flour or, just as effective and my own preference, fine oatmeal, for thickening sweet and savoury sauces, gravy, soups and casseroles. Providing you stir it in immediately and constantly, oatmeal, unlike wheat flour, will blend into a sauce without needing the liaison of fat.

The texture of jumbo oats, particularly, and rolled porridge oats gives a real lift to salads of all kinds, tossed, perhaps, with apples, celery and dried fruits with a yoghurt and lemony dressing. Alternatively, the oats can form part of the dressing, tossed with the vinaigrette ingredients or blended to a smooth sauce.

TOASTED OATS
Topping a recipe with toasted oats adds lots of crunch and few calories. All that needs to be done is to grill the oats on a baking tray under moderate heat for 3-4 minutes, stirring often.

GROATS, THE ULTIMATE OATS
The whole oat grain, or oat groats, need to be soaked overnight, then drained before being cooked for 1¼-1½ hours in a large pan of boiling water or stock. Drain again after cooking.

Alternatively, the soaked and drained groats can be cooked as follows:
Oven: Heat a large ovenproof dish of water to boiling point, then add the groats, cover and cook in a fairly hot oven 190°C/375°F/Gas 5, for 1¾-2 hours.
Microwave cooker: Cook the groats and enough liquid to cover on HIGH for 14-16 minutes.
Slow cooker: Boil the groats in a large pan of liquid for 20 minutes, then transfer to a preheated slow cooker, and cook on HIGH for 8 hours.
Pressure cooker: Cook the groats for 20-35 minutes at HIGH pressure in 5cm/2 inches of water.

Once cooked, groats have the appearance and many of the characteristics of long-grain brown rice, and can be used in salads, risottos, pilafs, rissoles, stuffings and soups. As with other long, slow-cooking ingredients (pulses for instance), it makes sense to cook more than your immediate needs so that you have some ready at hand for all the other uses. They store perfectly in a lidded container in a refrigerator, or can be open frozen, then stored in a sealed polythene bag for up to 6 months.

PORRIDGE – BASIC COOKING METHODS

The thickness of porridge is a matter of personal taste. Proportions are best gauged by volume, in the proportion of one of oats to two-three of water or other liquid.

Cooking method	Rolled porridge oats	Jumbo oats	Pinhead (coarse) oatmeal	Medium oatmeal	Fine oatmeal
Direct heat	Heat oats and liquid to boiling point, then boil for 1 minute. Remove from heat. Set aside for 5 minutes.	Heat oats and liquid to boiling point, then simmer for 10 minutes.	Soak oatmeal in water overnight, then heat to boiling point, and simmer for 40-60 minutes.	Soak oatmeal in water overnight, then heat to boiling point, and simmer for 15-20 minutes.	Heat oatmeal and liquid to boiling point, then simmer for 2 minutes.
Double boiler	Heat oats and liquid to boiling point, then cook for 10 minutes.	Heat oats and liquid to boiling point, then cook for 20 minutes.	Soak oatmeal in water overnight, then heat to boiling point, and cook for 1-1¼ hours.	Soak oatmeal in water overnight, then heat to boiling point, and cook for 30-40 minutes.	Heat oatmeal and liquid to boiling point, then cook for 5 minutes.
Oven	Heat water to boiling point, then add oats, cover and cook in a fairly hot oven, 200°C/400°F/Gas 6, for 10-15 minutes.	Heat water to boiling point, then add oats, cover and cook in a fairly hot oven, 200°C/400°F/Gas 6, for 20-25 minutes.	Heat water to boiling point, then add oatmeal, cover and cook in a fairly hot oven, 200°C/400°F/Gas 6, for 40-50 minutes.	Heat water to boiling point, then add oatmeal, cover and cook in a fairly hot oven, 200°C/400°F/Gas 6, for 20-25 minutes.	Heat water to boiling point, then add oatmeal, cover and cook in a fairly hot oven, 200°C/400°F/Gas 6, for 10-15 minutes.
Microwave cooker	Cook the oats and liquid on HIGH for 4 minutes.	Cook the oats and liquid on HIGH for 5½-6 minutes.	Leave oatmeal and liquid to stand for 2-3 hours, then cook on HIGH for 7-8 minutes. Stir or whisk vigorously before serving.	Cook oatmeal and liquid on HIGH for 3½-4 minutes, stirring vigorously, then cook for a further 3½-4 minutes.	Cook oatmeal and liquid on HIGH for 2-2½ minutes, stirring vigorously, then cook for a further 2-2½ minutes.
Slow cooker	Heat oats and liquid to boiling point in a pan, then transfer to a preheated cooker, and cook on LOW for 8 hours.	Heat oats and liquid to boiling point in a pan, then transfer to a preheated cooker, and cook on LOW for 8 hours.	Soak oatmeal in water overnight, then heat to boiling point in a pan, and boil for 3 minutes. Transfer to a preheated cooker, and cook on LOW for 8 hours.	Soak oatmeal in water overnight, then heat to boiling point in a pan. Transfer to a preheated cooker, and cook on LOW for 8 hours.	Heat oatmeal and liquid to boiling point in a pan, then transfer to a preheated cooker, and cook on LOW for 8 hours.
Vacuum flask or 'hay' box insulated covered container	Heat oats and liquid to boiling point. Transfer to flask or other container. Cover, set aside for 1 hour, or overnight.	Heat oats and liquid to boiling point. Transfer to flask or other container. Cover, set aside for 1 hour, or overnight.	Heat oatmeal and liquid to boiling point, then boil for 5 minutes. Transfer to flask or other container. Cover, set aside for 2 hours, or overnight.	Heat oatmeal and liquid to boiling point, then boil for 5 minutes. Transfer to flask or other container. Cover, set aside for 1½ hours, or overnight.	Heat oatmeal and liquid to boiling point, then boil for 5 minutes. Transfer to flask or other container. Cover, set aside for 1 hour, or overnight.

Hello, Sunshine!

People in Northern Europe have been going to work on a bowl of oats for centuries. In Scotland, it is made from oatmeal, and stirred, almost ritually, with a wooden stick called a spurtle. There they eat it well salted and unsweetened, and dipped, spoon by spoon, into a bowl of milk; not swimming in hot or cold milk and sprinkled with honey or dried fruits, as the English tend to prefer it.

Perhaps our ancestors knew by instinct what medical research now shows – that oats are a good source of protein and carbohydrates, and are relatively low in fat and calories. A great way to put vigour into the day and to enjoy also at all times.

Health-food enthusiasts have been giving the cereal a popularity boom, since jumbo oats and rolled porridge oats are the main basic ingredients of muesli, to which you can add your own choice of seeds, nuts, fresh and dried fruits and even vegetables.

But don't stop there! Oats make a tasty and nutritious addition to yoghurt, milk and fruit shakes; a deliciously gooey topping to grilled grapefruit; a crisp and crunchy 'jacket' for grilled fish, and a crumbly textured biscuit to serve with savoury dishes or cheese.

SCOTS PORRIDGE

100g/4 oz medium **or** pinhead oatmeal
900ml/1½ pints water
salt

Put the oatmeal and water into a small pan, stir well, cover and leave to soak overnight.

Add the salt, and heat slowly to boiling point stirring all the time. Simmer for 15-20 minutes if using medium oatmeal and for 40-60 minutes for pinhead oatmeal. Stir occasionally. Serve at once, in heated bowls.

Note The traditional Scots way is to dip a spoonful of porridge into an individual bowl of cold milk, and to sprinkle more salt over it. In other regions, porridge is served with hot or cold milk poured on to it, and sweetened with honey or brown sugar.

To cook different types of oats, see page 14.

FRUITY PORRIDGE

100g/4 oz rolled porridge oats **or** jumbo oats
900ml/1½ pints water
salt
3 × 15ml spoons/3 tablespoons low-fat yoghurt

2 × 15ml spoons/2 tablespoons sultanas
2 × 15ml spoons/2 tablespoons currants
8 dried apricots, chopped
2 × 15ml spoons/2 tablespoons Brazil nuts, chopped

Put the oats and water into a small pan, stir well, cover and leave to soak overnight.

Add the salt, and heat slowly to boiling point, stirring all the time. Simmer for 10 minutes, stirring occasionally. Remove from the heat and beat in the yoghurt, then stir in the dried fruits and nuts. Serve at once, in heated bowls.

Serve with milk, buttermilk or more yoghurt.

MUESLI BASE

MAKES 550g/1¼ lb

300g/10 oz rolled porridge oats
50g/2 oz jumbo oats
50g/2 oz oatbran and oatgerm
50g/2 oz sunflower seeds
100g/4 oz chopped mixed nuts

Mix together all the ingredients. Store in an airtight container in a cool place.

Note The muesli base will keep for several months if stored as above.

FRESH FRUIT MUESLI

SERVES 2

1 dessert apple, peeled, cored and chopped
1 orange, divided into segments, pith and skin removed
1 banana, thinly sliced
juice of 1 orange
8 × 15ml spoons/8 tablespoons Muesli base
2-4 × 15ml spoons/2-4 tablespoons soft fruit, hulled and picked over,
eg blackberries or strawberries (optional)

Toss the apple, orange and banana in the orange juice. Put the muesli into serving bowls, and scatter the fruit on top, if used.

Serve with skimmed milk, buttermilk, low-fat yoghurt or unsweetened fruit juice.

DRIED FRUIT MUESLI

16 × 15ml spoons/16 tablespoons Muesli base (page 16)
50g/2 oz dried apricot pieces
25g/1 oz fig paste, chopped
25g/1 oz dried banana 'chips'
50g/2 oz dried stoned dates, chopped
50g/2 oz sultanas
25g/1 oz mixed candied peel, chopped
juice of 1 lemon

Mix together the muesli and dried fruits. Sprinkle each serving with lemon juice, and serve with skimmed milk, buttermilk, low-fat yoghurt or unsweetened fruit juice.

Note The dry mixture can be stored in an airtight container.

VEGETABLE MUESLI

SERVES 2

50g/2 oz stoned dried dates, chopped
1 medium carrot, grated
2 stalks tender celery, thinly sliced
50g/2 oz button mushrooms, thinly sliced
½ small bulb fennel, thinly sliced, if available
1 × 15ml spoon/1 tablespoon pumpkin seeds
8 × 15ml spoons/8 tablespoons Muesli base (page 16)

Stir the fruit, vegetables and pumpkin seeds into the muesli.
Serve with buttermilk or low-fat yoghurt.

Note To save time in the morning, the vegetables can be prepared overnight and stored in a small, lidded container in a refrigerator.

TOASTED MUESLI

SERVES 12

1 recipe quantity Muesli base (page 16)
50g/2 oz shredded coconut
4 × 15ml spoons/4 tablespoons clear honey
2 × 15ml spoons/2 tablespoons sunflower oil
100g/4 oz seedless raisins

Mix the muesli and coconut. Melt the honey and oil in a pan, pour this over the muesli, and mix well. Spread the mixture on baking trays. Bake in a warm oven, 160°C/325°F/Gas 3, for 25 minutes until browned, turning the mixture frequently with a wooden spoon so that it cooks evenly. Cool completely, then stir in the raisins.
Serve with skimmed milk, buttermilk or low-fat yoghurt.

Note Store the dry mixture in a lidded container in a cool place.

MORNING COCKTAIL

75g/3 oz rolled porridge oats
300ml/½ pint skimmed milk
50g/2 oz dried apricot pieces
150ml/¼ pint water
2 bananas, sliced
1 dessert apple, peeled, cored and
chopped

juice of 1½ oranges
1 × 5ml spoon/1 teaspoon grated orange
rind
50g/2 oz hazelnuts

DECORATION

orange wedges

Soak the oats in the milk overnight. Soak the apricot pieces in the water overnight.
   Liquidize the oats, milk, apricots, water, bananas, apple, orange juice and orange rind and the hazelnuts in a blender, or press the apricots and banana through a sieve, grate the apple, finely chop the nuts and mix together all the ingredients. Pour into four glasses, and serve with orange wedges.

PEACH SUNDAY

SERVES 3-4

50g/2 oz medium oatmeal
300ml/½ pint low-fat yoghurt
150ml/¼ pint unsweetened pineapple juice
3 fresh peaches, skinned, stoned and chopped
2 eggs

DECORATION

2 × 15ml spoons/2 tablespoons rolled porridge oats, toasted

Stir the oatmeal into the yoghurt, cover and chill in a refrigerator overnight.
   Liquidize the oatmeal, yoghurt, pineapple juice, chopped peaches and eggs in a blender, or sieve the peaches, whisk the eggs lightly, and mix together all the ingredients. Pour the mixture into glasses, and sprinkle with the toasted oats. Stir, if liked, into the mixture just before drinking.

Variations
Other fresh fruits, according to season, can be substituted for the peaches.

OPPOSITE *Morning Cocktail*

FIRST-DOWN BISCUITS

MAKES 12

50g/2 oz medium oatmeal
150ml/¼ pint milk
50g/2 oz stoned dried dates, finely chopped
2 × 15ml spoons/2 tablespoons hot water

50g/2 oz oatbran and oatgerm
175g/6 oz wholewheat flour
1 × 15ml spoon/1 tablespoon sunflower oil
75g/3 oz sultanas
1 dessert apple, peeled, cored and grated

Soak the oatmeal in the milk for 30 minutes. Soak the dates in the hot water for 30 minutes, then mash them to a paste. Stir in the oatmeal and milk.

Mix together the oatbran and the flour, then stir in the oatmeal mixture and the remaining ingredients. Spread into a well greased 17.5 × 27.5cm/7 × 11 inch tin, and level the surface. Bake in a moderate oven, 180°C/350°F/Gas 4, for 20-25 minutes until golden-brown. Mark into 12 fingers, and leave to cool slightly in the tin. Cut out and cool on a wire rack. Store in an airtight tin.

Note These biscuits make a nutritious start to the day combined with an apple or orange.

OAT CAKES

MAKES 16

225g/8 oz rolled porridge oats **or** jumbo oats **plus** extra for rolling
100g/4 oz wholewheat flour
salt
1 × 5ml spoon/1 teaspoon baking powder
50g/2 oz sunflower margarine

Mix together the oats, flour, salt and baking powder. Rub in the margarine, and sprinkle with just enough water to make a firm dough.

Scatter some oats over a working surface, and knead the dough lightly. Roll it to a circle about 17.5cm/7 inch in diameter and 6mm/¼ inch thick. Using a plate as a guide, trim the dough to a neat round. Re-roll to form a second circle.

Place each dough round on a greased baking sheet, and cut into eight wedges. Bake in a moderate oven, 180°C/350°F/Gas 4, for 25 minutes until browned at the edges. Leave to cool slightly in the tin, then transfer to a wire rack. Serve spread with low-fat cheese and dried fruits.

OATMEAL BANNOCKS

MAKES 4

100g/4 oz medium oatmeal **plus** extra for rolling
a pinch of bicarbonate of soda
salt
2 × 5ml spoons/2 teaspoons sunflower margarine, melted
oil for greasing

Mix together the oatmeal, bicarbonate of soda and the salt. Stir in the margarine, then sprinkle on just enough hot water to make a stiff paste. Form the dough into a ball.

Scatter oatmeal over a working surface, and knead the dough lightly. Roll it to a circle about 6mm/¼ inch thick. Using a plate as a guide, trim the dough to a neat round, then cut it into quarters. Sprinkle a little oatmeal on top.

Cook the bannocks on a hot, lightly greased griddle or in a heavy frying pan over high heat for 3-4 minutes until the edges start to curl. Place under a moderate grill, and cook until the bannocks are crisp.

Serve hot or cold, with fish.

POTATO HOTCAKES

SERVES 2

900g/2 lb potatoes, peeled and grated
2 × 15ml spoons/2 tablespoons medium oatmeal
2 × 15ml spoons/2 tablespoons rolled porridge oats **or** jumbo oats
1 small onion, grated

1 × 5ml spoon/1 teaspoon dry English mustard
salt, freshly ground pepper
2 eggs, beaten
oil for greasing

Put the grated potato into a colander and press out the moisture, using a saucer. Alternatively, wring the potato in a clean tea-towel.

Mix the potato with the oatmeal, rolled oats, onion, mustard, salt and pepper. Beat in the eggs to form a thick paste consistency.

Drop heaped tablespoons of the mixture on to a lightly greased griddle or heavy frying pan, and fry over moderate heat for 2-3 minutes on each side until the hotcakes are evenly brown. Serve hot, with fish or grilled mushrooms and tomatoes.

STUFFED MUSHROOMS

450g/1 lb button mushrooms
2 × 15ml spoons/2 tablespoons olive oil
15g/½ oz sunflower margarine
1 small onion, finely chopped
50g/2 oz medium oatmeal
2 × 15ml spoons/2 tablespoons chopped parsley

2 × 15ml spoons/2 tablespoons chopped walnuts
salt, freshly ground pepper
50g/2 oz low-fat soft cheese

Pull out the mushroom caps and chop the stalks. Melt the oil and margarine in a pan, and fry the onion over moderate heat for 3 minutes, stirring occasionally. Stir in the chopped mushroom stalks, the oatmeal, parsley and walnuts, and season with salt and pepper. Beat in the cheese, then remove from the heat.

Place the mushrooms caps in a greased baking dish, hollow side up. Divide the filling between them, pressing it well into the caps. Cook in a fairly hot oven, 190°C/375°F/Gas 5, for 15-20 minutes until the filling is bubbling. Serve at once, with toast and, if you like, halved tomatoes baked in the oven at the same time.

GRILLED GRAPEFRUIT

4 grapefruit, halved and cut into sections
1 × 15ml spoon/1 tablespoon seedless raisins
a pinch of ground ginger
4 × 15ml spoons/4 tablespoons rolled porridge oats
1 × 15ml spoon/1 tablespoon clear honey, melted
2 × 15ml spoons/2 tablespoons orange juice

Place the grapefruit, cut sides up, on the grill pan. Press the raisins into the cavity left after removing the central core.

Mix together the ginger, oats, honey and orange juice in a bowl, and spread the mixture over the grapefruit. Grill the grapefruit over moderate heat until the topping is brown and crisp. Serve at once.

Oat Cakes (see page 20) go well with this hot and tangy breakfast dish.

OPPOSITE *Grilled Herrings* and *Oat Cakes* (*page 20*)

GRILLED HERRINGS

4 fresh herrings, heads removed, gutted
and cleaned
2 × 15ml spoons/2 tablespoons lemon
juice
salt, freshly ground pepper
2 × 15ml spoons/2 tablespoons fine
oatmeal
2 × 15ml spoons/2 tablespoons
sunflower oil

2 × 15ml spoons/2 tablespoons French
mustard
5 × 15ml spoons/5 tablespoons rolled
porridge oats **or** jumbo oats
4 × 15ml spoons/4 tablespoons
sunflower margarine, melted

GARNISH

lemon slices
sprigs dill

Sprinkle the inside of the herrings with lemon juice, and season with salt and pepper. Toss
the fish in the fine oatmeal to coat them.

Brush the fish with the oil, and grill under high heat for 3 minutes on each side. Brush
with the mustard, then press on the oats to coat them. Sprinkle with half the melted
margarine. Grill again for 3 minutes, turn the fish, sprinkle with the remaining margarine,
and grill for a further 3-4 minutes. Garnish with the lemon slices and dill. Serve at once,
with Oat Cakes (see page 20).

Time is the Essence

Everyone's so incredibly busy these days. I am for ever hearing people say that they haven't time to prepare and cook a meal because of this commitment or that. And, what's more, that there's scarcely time to grab something to eat before dashing out again. Which, of course, simply won't do!

But there's no denying the fact that the fast-food era is upon us. And even in the best regulated of households there are bound to be times when a quick single-course meal is the order of the day.

Quite unlike the other chapters, this section is a scrapbook of ideas for quick snacks and easy starters. Some of the recipes you can prepare in advance and leave ready to eat in a hurry, others you can whip up when you're more interested in having something tasty to eat, soon, than in the actual therapy of cooking.

Oats really come into their own at times like this. They add valuable nutrients and soluble – easily digestible – fibre, proving that the terms 'fast food' and 'junk food' are certainly not synonymous.

In pâtés, dips and savoury fillings, oatmeal is a useful extender, diluting strong flavours in the way that breadcrumbs do; but spooned straight from the pack, it's a good deal quicker. In egg dishes, oats can add both bulk and texture – they're amazingly good in pancakes – and help you produce satisfying dishes with a reduced cholesterol level. And in salads, especially the kind that make a meal, oats have just what it takes – crunch and eye appeal.

WIDE-OPEN SANDWICHES

MAKES **4**

2 medium bananas, mashed
2 × 15ml spoons/2 tablespoons fine oatmeal
50g/2 oz stoned dried dates, chopped
8 dried apricots, soaked, drained and chopped

4 × 5ml spoons/4 teaspoons lemon juice
4 slices Oat Bread (page 92)
1 dessert apple, cored and thinly sliced
1 peach, peeled, stoned and thinly sliced

GARNISH

sprigs watercress

Mix together the bananas, oatmeal, dates, apricots and half the lemon juice. Spread the mixture over one side of each slice of bread.

Toss the apple and peach slices in the remaining lemon juice, and arrange the fruit over the banana filling. Garnish with watercress.

Variations
Top the basic sandwich with other fresh fruits in season, eg raspberries, blackberries, sliced plums or pears.

STUFFED TOMATOES

4 large tomatoes

STUFFING

2 × 15ml spoons/2 tablespoons
sunflower oil
1 medium onion, finely chopped
2 cloves garlic, crushed
1 green pepper, de-seeded and finely
chopped

100g/4 oz button mushrooms, chopped
100g/4 oz chopped mixed nuts
25g/1 oz wholewheat breadcrumbs
50g/2 oz rolled porridge oats
2 × 15ml spoons/2 tablespoons chopped
parsley
salt, freshly ground pepper

Cut a thin slice from the top of each tomato. Use a teaspoon to scoop out and reserve the seeds, taking care not to pierce the 'walls'. Stand the tomatoes upside-down to drain.

Meanwhile, make the stuffing. Heat the oil in a pan, and cook the onion and garlic over moderate heat, stirring occasionally. Add the pepper, reserved tomato seeds and mushrooms, stir well and fry for 2 minutes. Stir in the nuts, breadcrumbs and oats, and stir over heat for 1 minute. Remove from the heat, stir in the parsley, and season with salt and pepper.

Stand the tomatoes in a baking dish. Spoon in the stuffing, and press it down firmly. Bake in a fairly hot oven, 190°C/375°F/Gas 5, for 25-30 minutes until bubbling. Serve hot.

Serve with a green or pulse salad.

MOUNTAIN OMELET

SERVES 2

1 × 15ml spoon/1 tablespoon sunflower
oil
1 medium onion, chopped
1 clove of garlic, crushed
2 small courgettes, diced
2 small cooked potatoes, peeled and
diced
2 tomatoes, skinned and chopped

3 eggs
1 × 15ml spoon/1 tablespoon water
6 × 15ml spoons/6 tablespoons rolled
porridge oats
salt, freshly ground pepper
a pinch of Cayenne pepper
2 × 15ml spoons/2 tablespoons grated
Edam cheese

Heat the oil in an omelet pan, then fry the onion, garlic, courgettes and potatoes over moderate heat for 3 minutes, stirring frequently. Stir in the tomatoes.

Beat the eggs with the water, then stir in 4 × 15ml spoons/4 tablespoons of the oats. Season with salt, pepper and the Cayenne pepper. Pour the egg mixture into the pan, and stir lightly with a fork. Cook until the base of the omelet is just set and the top is still moist.

Mix the cheese with the remainder of the oats. Sprinkle over the omelet, and grill it under moderate heat for about 30 seconds to set the top. Serve at once, with a salad. Alternatively turn it on to a plate, and leave to cool.

Note Cut into wedges and wrapped in foil, the cold omelet makes a good lunch-box alternative to sandwiches.

MUSHROOM SCRAMBLE

SERVES 3-4

350g/12 oz button mushrooms
2 × 15ml spoons/2 tablespoons olive oil
2 × 15ml spoons/2 tablespoons orange juice
1 × 5ml spoon/1 teaspoon grated orange rind
150ml/¼ pint dry cider
3 × 15ml spoons/3 tablespoons red wine

2 cloves garlic, finely chopped
1 bay leaf
salt, freshly ground pepper
2 large tomatoes, skinned and chopped
2 × 15ml spoons/2 tablespoons fine oatmeal
2 × 15ml spoons/2 tablespoons chopped parsley

Trim the mushroom stalks level with the cap. (You can use the stalks in soup or a sauce.)
Put the oil, orange juice and orange rind, the cider, wine, garlic and bay leaf into a pan, and heat to boiling point. Season with salt and pepper, then simmer for 5 minutes. Add the mushrooms, and simmer for 5 minutes. Stir in the tomatoes and oatmeal, and simmer for a further 3 minutes. Season to taste, then stir in the parsley. Serve warm, with wholewheat bread.

MUSHROOM PÂTÉ

25g/1 oz sunflower margarine
2 small onions, chopped
2 cloves garlic, crushed
225g/8 oz field mushrooms, chopped
125g/5 oz cottage cheese
40g/1½ oz medium oatmeal
1 × 5ml spoon/1 teaspoon soy sauce
1 × 15ml spoon/1 tablespoon medium sherry

salt, freshly ground pepper
2 × 15ml spoons/2 tablespoons chopped parsley

GARNISH

mushroom slices

Melt the margarine in a pan, and cook the onion and garlic over moderate heat for 3 minutes, stirring occasionally. Add the mushrooms, stir well, then lower the heat. Continue frying for 10 minutes, stirring frequently, then lift them out with a slotted spoon.
Put the vegetables in a blender with the cheese, oatmeal, soy sauce and sherry, and process until the purée is smooth. Alternatively, press the vegetables and cheese through a sieve, and mix with the remaining ingredients. Season the purée with salt and pepper, then stir in the parsley. Spoon it into four individual ramekin dishes, and level the surface. Cover with clingfilm, and chill overnight in a refrigerator. Garnish with the mushroom slices.

OPPOSITE *Mushroom Pâté and Cheese and Nut Pâté*

CHEESE AND NUT PÂTÉ

SERVES 6-8

225g/8 oz low-fat soft cheese
50g/2 oz toasted hazelnuts, coarsely
ground
50g/2 oz medium oatmeal
2 × 15ml spoons/2 tablespoons chopped
parsley
1 medium carrot, grated
1 stalk of tender celery, finely chopped

½ small green pepper, de-seeded and
finely chopped
2 spring onions, finely chopped
salt, freshly ground pepper

GARNISH

sprigs watercress

Mix together all the ingredients, and season to taste with salt and pepper. Press the mixture into a dish, and level the surface. Cover with foil, and chill for 2 hours or overnight. Garnish with the watercress sprigs.

Serve with wholewheat crackers or toast.

Variation
Pack the pâté into de-seeded peppers, wrap them in foil, and chill. Serve thinly sliced, as an unusual first course.

SALAD LAYER

SERVES 4-6

50g/2 oz rolled porridge oats **or** jumbo oats
50g/2 oz sunflower seeds
50g/2 oz stoned dried dates, sliced
50g/2 oz dried apricots, sliced
25g/1 oz currants
½ small red cabbage, thinly sliced
2 medium carrots, grated
2 small onions, sliced into rings
1 red pepper, de-seeded and thinly sliced

1 green pepper, de-seeded and thinly sliced
2 dessert apples, cored and thinly sliced

DRESSING

4 × 15ml spoons/4 tablespoons olive oil
4 spring onions, finely chopped
2 × 15ml spoons/2 tablespoons unsweetened pineapple juice
salt, freshly ground pepper

Mix together the oats, sunflower seeds, dates, apricots and currants, and put to one side. Mix together the dressing ingredients until well blended.

In a bowl – a glass one is ideal – make layers of cabbage and carrots, cabbage and onion rings, cabbage and pepper, cabbage and apples, then finally a layer of cabbage. Sprinkle the oats mixture between each layer. Pour the dressing over the salad, but do not toss it.

Serve with wholemeal rolls spread with cottage cheese.

VEGETABLE MEDLEY

25g/1 oz sunflower margarine
2 × 15ml spoons/2 tablespoons sunflower oil
2 medium onions, thinly sliced
2 medium leeks, thinly sliced
2 medium carrots, thinly sliced
2 medium courgettes, sliced
2 large tomatoes, skinned and sliced

50g/2 oz jumbo oats
300ml/½ pint chicken **or** vegetable stock
50g/2 oz sultanas
50g/2 oz hard cheese, diced
salt, freshly ground pepper
4 × 15ml spoons/4 tablespoons toasted almonds

Heat the margarine and oil in a pan, and cook the onions and leeks over moderate heat for 3 minutes, stirring occasionally. Add the carrots, courgettes and tomatoes, then stir well, and cook for a further 1-2 minutes. Stir in the oats. Pour on the stock, stir well and heat to boiling point. Cover the pan and simmer for 20 minutes. Add the sultanas and cheese, and season with salt and pepper. Stir with a fork, and cook for a further 2-3 minutes until the cheese has melted. Scatter with the almonds. Serve hot.

Serve with wholewheat bread and a salad.

CAULIFLOWER CHEESE CASSEROLE

1 cauliflower, cut into florets
225g/8 oz calabrese **or** broccoli, cut into florets
salt, freshly ground pepper
300ml/½ pint low-fat yoghurt
2 × 15ml/2 tablespoons wholewheat flour

225g/8 oz cottage cheese, sieved
a pinch of Cayenne pepper
25g/1 oz sunflower margarine, melted
50g/2 oz Edam cheese, grated
100g/4 oz rolled porridge oats
25g/1 oz sunflower seeds

Partly cook the cauliflower and calabrese in boiling salted water for 5-7 minutes until they are barely tender, then drain.

Gradually stir the yoghurt into the flour. Heat it over low heat, stirring all the time, until it simmers. Remove from the heat and beat in the cheese. Season with salt, pepper and Cayenne pepper.

Arrange the vegetables in a casserole, and pour over the sauce. Mix together the margarine, grated cheese, oats and seeds, and sprinkle this over the sauce. Cook the casserole, uncovered, in a fairly hot oven, 200°C/400°F/Gas 6, for 30-35 minutes until bubbling. Serve hot.

Serve with a green or tomato salad.

ABERDEEN PATTIES

MAKES 4

175g/6 oz smoked haddock fillet
300ml/½ pint skimmed milk
a few parsley stalks
1 bay leaf
a sprig of thyme
100g/4 oz rolled porridge oats
1 × 2.5ml spoon/½ teaspoon curry powder
salt, freshly ground pepper

2 × 15ml spoons/2 tablespoons chopped parsley
fine oatmeal for dusting
1 egg, beaten

GARNISH

lemon twists
stuffed olives, sliced

Put the fish into a frying pan with the milk, parsley stalks, bay leaf and thyme. Heat slowly to boiling point, then simmer for 10 minutes. Lift out the fish, skin it, discard any bones and flake it. Strain the milk.

Stir 75g/3 oz of the oats into the milk. Heat slowly to boiling point, then simmer for 4 minutes, stirring frequently. Stir in the curry powder, and season with salt and pepper. Remove from the heat and leave to cool. Stir in the flaked fish and the chopped parsley.

Dust your hands with fine oatmeal, and divide the mixture into four pieces. Shape each one into a round, and press it flat. Dip them in the beaten egg and then in the reserved oats.

Fry the patties in a non-stick pan over moderate heat until golden-brown on each side. Serve hot, garnished with lemon twists and olive slices.

Note Tiny new potatoes and fresh beans are a good accompaniment.

CHICKEN PATTIES

MAKES 4

350g/12 oz raw chicken, minced
1 slice of lean bacon, without rinds, minced
1 small onion, finely chopped
8 dried apricots, soaked and drained, finely chopped
4 × 15ml spoons/4 tablespoons medium oatmeal
1-2 × 15ml spoons/1-2 tablespoons oatbran and oatgerm (optional)

2 × 15ml spoons/2 tablespoons chopped parsley
salt, freshly ground pepper
1 egg, beaten
fine oatmeal for dusting
oil for frying (optional)

GARNISH

onion rings
cucumber slices
lettuce

Mix together the chicken, bacon, onion, apricots, medium oatmeal, oatbran and the parsley. Season with salt and pepper, and bind to a thick paste with the beaten egg.

Dust your hands with fine oatmeal, and divide the mixture into four pieces. Shape each one to form an oval, and press it flat. Dust the patties in oatmeal to cover them.

Brush a frying pan with oil, if necessary. Fry the patties over moderate heat for 5 minutes on each side until they are brown. Serve at once, garnished with raw onion rings, cucumber slices and lettuce.

CHICKEN PANCAKES

MAKES 4

100g/4 oz wholewheat flour
40g/1½ oz rolled porridge oats
salt, freshly ground pepper
2 eggs
300ml/½ pint skimmed milk
oil for frying (optional)
40g/1½ oz Edam cheese, grated

FILLING

225g/8 oz low-fat soft cheese
225g/8 oz cooked chicken, diced
2 × 15ml spoons/2 tablespoons chopped parsley
a pinch of Cayenne pepper
a pinch of paprika

Mix together the flour, porridge oats, salt and pepper. Beat in the eggs, and gradually pour on the milk, beating all the time.

Lightly brush an omelet pan with oil, if necessary. Heat the pan over moderate heat, and pour in just enough of the batter to cover the base. Shake the pan, and cook the batter for 2-3 minutes until it bubbles and the underside is brown. Flip or toss the pancake, and cook until the other side is brown. Keep the cooked pancake warm while cooking the remaining batter.

To make the filling, stir together the soft cheese and chicken, stir in the parsley, and season with Cayenne pepper and paprika.

Fill the pancakes with the mixture, and roll them up. Arrange them in a single layer in a shallow flameproof dish, and sprinkle the grated cheese on top. Grill the pancakes under moderate heat until the cheese is brown. Serve at once.

Serve with a salad or with grilled tomatoes.

OPPOSITE *Chicken Patties*

Pot Luck

Oats have a long association with warming, welcoming fare, simmering on the stove in the meat, fish or vegetable broth that constitutes the 'pot luck' of homely cooking. Scotch broth, at the very heart of Northern tradition, is a fine example, in which rolled porridge oats are cooked with hardy root vegetables in a stock flavoured with meat. The dish is not only satisfying, tasty and economical, it also demonstrates one of the principals of healthy cooking – that a little meat can go a long way. We do not have to load our plates with saturated animal fats to enjoy the taste.

In all the various forms, oats are a vegetable soup and stew ingredient, whether using groats to absorb surrounding flavours, or oatmeal and rolled oats to thicken stocks.

Mix rolled oats with flour or breadcrumbs to make the kind of dumplings that bob airily to the surface of the broth. Toast oat bread and use it as a garnish or topping – it is especially good spread with crushed garlic. Toast rolled oats with chopped nuts, or mix them with fresh herbs for a quick and easy-sprinkle garnish, or crumble oat cakes to float on top of thick puréed soups.

When it comes to pot luck, oats have a well-deserved air of importance.

CELERIAC SOUP

SERVES 6-8

225g/8 oz celeriac, chopped
2 large carrots, diced
1 litre/1¾ pints chicken stock
300ml/½ pint skimmed milk
40g/1½ oz medium oatmeal
salt, freshly ground pepper
1 × 2.5ml spoon/½ teaspoon celery seeds

2 × 15ml spoons/2 tablespoons chopped parsley

GARNISH

2 × 5ml/2 teaspoons celery seeds
2 × 15ml spoons/2 tablespoons jumbo oats, toasted
a few celery leaves

Cook the celeriac and carrots in the stock for 20 minutes until tender, then liquidize them in a blender. Alternatively, rub them through a sieve, or purée them in a vegetable mill. Return the purée to the pan, and pour on the milk and oatmeal, stirring all the time. Season with salt, pepper and celery seeds, then heat slowly to boiling point. Just before serving, stir in the chopped parsley. Garnish with the celery seeds, oats and a few herb leaves.

CORN CHANDLERS SOUP

15g/½ oz sunflower margarine
1 × 15ml spoon/1 tablespoon olive oil
1 medium onion, chopped
225g/8 oz carrots, sliced slantways
2 medium leeks (white part only), sliced slantways
2 stalks celery, thinly sliced
125g/5 oz 'soup mix' (dried split peas, lentils, barley and oatmeal)
25g/1 oz jumbo oats **or** rolled porridge oats

900ml/1½ pints chicken stock
1 × 5ml spoon/1 teaspoon mixed dried herbs
1 bouquet garni
salt, freshly ground pepper

GARNISH

grated carrot
sprigs watercress

Heat the margarine and oil in a pan, and fry the onion, carrots, leeks and celery over moderate heat for 2 minutes, stirring all the time. Add the soup mix, oats, stock, herbs and bouquet garni, and stir well. Heat to boiling point, and boil for 10 minutes, then cover the pan and simmer for 40 minutes. Discard the bouquet garni. Season with salt and pepper, and sprinkle the soup with the grated carrot. Garnish with the watercress. Serve hot.

DUTCH DAIRY SOUP

450g/1 lb potatoes, peeled and cubed
900ml/1½ pints chicken stock
15g/½ oz sunflower margarine
1 large onion, chopped
2 cloves garlic, finely chopped
2 stalks celery, thinly sliced
4 × 15ml spoons/4 tablespoons pinhead oatmeal
1 large carrot, diced
1 small white turnip, diced
1 × 2.5ml spoon/½ teaspoon dried thyme

salt, freshly ground pepper
150ml/¼ pint low-fat soured cream
2 × 15ml spoons/2 tablespoons chopped parsley

GARNISH

8 small rounds Oat Bread (page 92)
50g/2 oz Edam cheese, grated
2 × 15ml spoons/2 tablespoons rolled porridge oats

Cook the potatoes in the stock until tender, then liquidize them in a blender or press them through a sieve.

Melt the margarine in a pan, and fry the onion, garlic and celery over moderate heat for 3 minutes, stirring frequently. Pour on the potato purée, then add the oatmeal, carrot, turnip and thyme, and stir well. Heat to boiling point, then cover the pan and simmer for 15-20 minutes until the vegetables are only just tender. Season the soup with salt and pepper, then stir in the soured cream and parsley, and heat slowly.

To make the garnish, toast the bread on both sides. Mix the grated cheese and oats, and spread them on the toast. Place under moderate heat, and cook until the cheese melts.

Float the toasted cheese on the soup, and serve at once.

TWO MUSHROOM SOUP

100g/4 oz button mushrooms
15g/½ oz sunflower margarine
1 medium onion, sliced
100g/4 oz field mushrooms, chopped
3 × 15ml spoons/3 tablespoons fine oatmeal
600ml/1 pint chicken stock
300ml/½ pint skimmed milk

1 × 15ml spoon/1 tablespoon lemon juice
1 × 15ml spoon/1 tablespoon mushroom ketchup
salt, freshly ground pepper
4 × 15ml spoons/4 tablespoons low-fat yoghurt

Chop 50g/2 oz button mushrooms and slice the remainder. Melt the margarine in a pan, and fry the onion and chopped button and field mushrooms over low heat for 7-8 minutes, stirring frequently. Stir in the oatmeal, and cook for 1 minute. Slowly pour on the stock and the milk, stirring all the time. Stir in the lemon juice and mushroom ketchup, and season with salt and pepper. Heat slowly to boiling point, then cover and simmer for 10 minutes. Swirl the yoghurt on top of the soup just before serving, then add the sliced mushrooms. Serve hot.

Variation
For a smooth soup, liquidize the vegetables and liquid in a blender, or press the vegetables through a sieve. Return the purée to the pan, and re-heat gently.

NORTHERN GAZPACHO

300ml/½ pint tomato juice
1 × 15ml spoon/1 tablespoon concentrated tomato purée
2 × 15ml spoons/2 tablespoons cider vinegar
150ml/¼ pint chicken stock
1 × 5ml spoon/1 teaspoon Worcestershire sauce
225g/8 oz tomatoes, skinned and sliced
salt, freshly ground pepper
1 small onion, finely chopped
1 leek (white part only), finely chopped

¼ cucumber, finely diced
1 red pepper, de-seeded and chopped
4 × 15ml spoons/4 tablespoons jumbo oats
2 × 15ml spoons/2 tablespoons chopped parsley
1 × 15ml spoon/1 tablespoon snipped chives

GARNISH

2 Oat Cakes (page 20), crumbled

Liquidize the tomato juice, tomato purée, vinegar, stock, sauce and tomatoes in a blender. Alternatively, rub the tomatoes through a sieve, and mix them with the liquid ingredients. Season the soup with salt and pepper. Stir in the prepared vegetables and the oats, then cover and chill for at least 1 hour.

Just before serving, stir in the herbs, and sprinkle with the oat cake crumbs. Serve in chilled bowls.

OPPOSITE *Lemon Soup, Lamb Broth with Oat Dumplings (page 40) and Northern Gazpacho*

LEMON SOUP

100g/4 oz yellow split peas, soaked and drained
25g/1 oz medium oatmeal
1 × 15ml spoon/1 tablespoon oatbran and oatgerm (optional)
1 medium onion, finely chopped
2 stalks celery, thinly sliced
grated rind of 1 lemon
juice of 1½ lemons

1 × 2.5ml spoon/½ teaspoon ground turmeric
1 litre/1¾ pints chicken stock (approx)
salt, freshly ground pepper

GARNISH

spring onions, sliced
lemon slices

Put the split peas, oatmeal, oatbran, onion, celery, lemon rind and juice, turmeric and stock into a pan, and heat to boiling point. Cover the pan, and simmer for 1 hour, adjusting the liquid as necessary. Season with salt and pepper. Stir the soup well, and sprinkle with the sliced onion. Float the lemon slices on top. Serve hot.

SCOTS OATMEAL SOUP

15g/½ oz sunflower margarine
1 large onion, finely chopped
4 × 15ml spoons/4 tablespoons medium oatmeal
600ml/1 pint chicken stock
a few stalks parsley
300ml/½ pint buttermilk

salt, freshly ground pepper
2 egg yolks, beaten

GARNISH

2 × 15ml spoons/2 tablespoons chopped parsley

Melt the margarine in a pan, and cook the onion over moderate heat for 3 minutes, stirring once or twice. Stir in the oatmeal, and cook for 1 minute. Slowly pour on the stock, stirring all the time, then add the parsley stalks. Heat to boiling point, then cover the pan and simmer for 30 minutes. Discard the parsley.

Liquidize the soup in a blender, or rub the mixture through a sieve. Return the purée to the pan, slowly pour on the buttermilk, and heat slowly to boiling point. Season with salt and pepper. Pour a little of the soup on to the egg yolks, then pour them into the soup, and heat over low heat. Serve hot, garnished with the parsley.

MEDITERRANEAN CHOWDER

2 × 15ml spoons/2 tablespoons olive oil
1 large onion, thinly sliced
4 stalks celery, thinly sliced
2 cloves garlic, finely chopped
450g/1 lb tomatoes, skinned
2 bay leaves
225g/8 oz potatoes, peeled and diced
600ml/1 pint fish **or** vegetable stock
2 × 15ml spoons/2 tablespoons concentrated tomato purée

675g/1½ lb white fish fillets, skinned, boned and cut into 3.75cm/1½ inch squares
2 × 15ml spoons/2 tablespoons chopped parsley
100g/4 oz shelled cooked prawns
salt, freshly ground pepper
4 cloves garlic, crushed
4 slices Oat Bread (page 92)
1 small leek (white part only) thinly sliced into rings

Heat the oil in a pan, and fry the onion, celery and garlic over moderate heat for 3 minutes, stirring occasionally. Add the tomatoes, bay leaves, potatoes, stock and tomato purée, and stir well. Heat to boiling point, then cover and simmer for 10 minutes. Add the fish and chopped parsley, then heat to boiling point. Cover and simmer for 10 minutes, then add the prawns, and season with salt and pepper. Cover and simmer for a further 5 minutes.

Rub the crushed garlic into the bread slices, then cut the bread into small squares. Place in the bottom of a heated serving dish, and pour on the chowder. Scatter the leeks on top.

COCK-A-LEEKIE

SERVES 6

1.35kg/3 lb chicken, including giblets
1 bouquet garni
8 medium leeks, cut into 2.5cm/1 inch slices
8 × 15ml spoons/8 tablespoons jumbo oats

12 prunes, soaked, drained and stoned
salt, freshly ground pepper

GARNISH

chopped parsley

Skin the chicken, then put it into a pan with the giblets, bouquet garni and half the leeks. Cover with water, and heat slowly to boiling point. Skim off any fat and foam that rises to the surface. Cover the pan and simmer for 1½ hours.

Remove the chicken from the stock, and leave to cool, then cut the meat from the bones, and cut it into chunks.

Strain the stock and discard the vegetables and giblets. Measure 1.2 litres/2 pints, and return it to the pan, then add the remaining leeks, the oats and prunes. Cover the pan and simmer for 15 minutes. Add the chicken, then season with salt and pepper, and heat gently. Serve hot, garnished with the parsley.

Oat Cakes (see page 20) are a good accompaniment.

SCOTCH BROTH

SERVES 6-8

450g/1 lb stewing beef, chopped
1.8 litres/3 pints water
225g/8 oz swede, diced
2 medium carrots, thinly sliced
1 large onion, chopped
1 leek (white part only), thinly sliced
1 bay leaf
100g/4 oz white cabbage, shredded
40g/1½ oz rolled porridge oats

1 × 15ml spoon/1 tablespoon concentrated tomato purée
salt, freshly ground pepper
2 × 15ml spoons/2 tablespoons chopped parsley

GARNISH

1 dessert apple, cored and thinly sliced

Fry the beef in a non-stick pan over moderate heat, stirring frequently, until the fat runs. Lift out the meat with a slotted spoon, and discard the fat. Return the meat to the pan. Pour on the water, and heat to boiling point. Skim off any fat and foam that rises to the surface. Cover the pan and simmer for 1 hour, then skim again. Add the swede, carrots, onion, leek and bay leaf, and heat to boiling point. Cover the pan and simmer for a further 1 hour. Add the cabbage, then stir in the tomato purée. Add the oats, and season with salt and pepper. Heat to boiling point, then cover the pan and simmer for 10 minutes. Discard the bay leaf, and season to taste, then stir in the parsley. Garnish the soup – in an un-Scots way! – with the apple slices. Serve hot.

GOULASH SOUP

SERVES 6

350g/12 oz lean beef, minced
1 large onion, chopped
3 × 15ml spoons/3 tablespoons medium oatmeal
1 × 15ml spoon/1 tablespoon paprika
1 × 2.5ml spoon/½ teaspoon caraway seeds
1 clove of garlic, crushed
400g/14 oz canned tomatoes
600ml/1 pint beef stock

1 × 15ml spoon/1 tablespoon concentrated tomato purée
1 red pepper, de-seeded and chopped
3 × 15ml spoons/3 tablespoons jumbo oats
225g/8 oz potatoes, peeled and cubed
salt, freshly ground pepper
150ml/¼ pint low-fat yoghurt
2 × 15ml spoons/2 tablespoons chopped parsley

Fry the beef in a non-stick pan over moderate heat, stirring all the time, until the fat runs. Lift out the meat with a slotted spoon, and discard the fat. Return the meat to the pan, then stir in the onion, oatmeal, paprika, caraway seeds and garlic, and cook for 2 minutes, stirring frequently. Add the tomatoes and their juice, and the stock, and heat slowly to boiling point. Cover the pan and simmer for 30 minutes. Stir in the tomato purée, red pepper, oats and potatoes, and season with salt and pepper. Cover the pan and cook for a further 15 minutes. Season to taste. Skim off any fat from the top of the soup. Swirl the yoghurt over the top of the soup just before serving, and sprinkle with the parsley.

CHILLI POT

125g/5 oz dried red kidney beans, soaked and drained (see **Note**)
125g/5 oz oat groats, soaked and drained
225g/8 oz lean beef, minced
2 × 15ml spoons/2 tablespoons sunflower oil
2 medium onions, sliced
2 green peppers, de-seeded and sliced
2 red peppers, de-seeded and sliced
4 stalks celery, thinly sliced
2 red chillis, de-seeded and chopped

2 × 15ml spoons/2 tablespoons medium oatmeal
1 × 15ml spoon/1 tablespoon oatbran and oatgerm (optional)
1 × 15ml spoon/1 tablespoon paprika
1 × 2.5ml spoon/½ teaspoon Cayenne pepper
300ml/½ pint beef stock
2 medium carrots, diced
salt, freshly ground pepper
2 × 15ml spoons/2 tablespoons chopped coriander leaves **or** parsley

Boil the kidney beans briskly in fresh water for at least 10 minutes, then cook for 50 minutes. Meanwhile, cook the groats in a separate pan of boiling water for 1 hour. Drain the beans and groats.

Fry the beef in a non-stick pan over moderate heat, stirring all the time, until the fat runs. Remove the meat with a slotted spoon, and discard the fat.

Heat the oil in a flameproof casserole, and fry the onions, peppers, celery and chillis over moderate heat for 4 minutes, stirring frequently. Add the meat, oatmeal, oatbran, paprika and Cayenne pepper, stir well and cook for 1 minute. Pour on the stock, then add the beans, groats and carrots. Heat to boiling point, stir well, then cover the pan. Simmer for 45 minutes, then season with salt and pepper, and stir in the herbs. Serve hot.

Note It is important to discard the draining water used for soaking the kidney beans.

OPPOSITE *Chilli Pot*

LAMB BROTH WITH OAT DUMPLINGS

SERVES 4-6

675g/1½ lb scrag end of lamb
1.5 litres/2½ pints water
225g/8 oz oat groats, soaked and drained
4 leeks (white part only), sliced
8 small carrots, cut into chunks
4 stalks celery, cut into chunks
1 small turnip, diced
salt, freshly ground pepper
2 × 15ml spoons/2 tablespoons chopped
parsley

DUMPLINGS

50g/2 oz wholewheat flour
25g/1 oz oatbran and oatgerm
salt, freshly ground pepper
25g/1 oz sunflower margarine
2-3 × 15ml spoons/2-3 tablespoons water
2 × 15ml spoons/2 tablespoons rolled
porridge oats

Put the lamb, water and groats in a pan. Heat slowly to boiling point, then skim off any fat and foam that rises to the top. Cover and simmer for 1½ hours, then skim again. Add the vegetables, and season with salt and pepper, then cover and simmer for a further hour.

Lift out the meat and bones with a slotted spoon. Discard the bones. Return the meat to the pan, and leave overnight if possible. Lift off any fat that has settled on top of the pan.

To make the dumplings, mix together the flour, oatbran and oatgerm, salt and pepper, then rub in the margarine. Sprinkle on enough water to make a firm dough. Shape the dough into small rounds, then roll them in the oats.

Re-heat the broth until boiling, and season to taste. Add the dumplings, and simmer for 10 minutes, then stir in the chopped parsley. Serve at once.

LAMB REVITHIA

125g/5 oz dried chick-peas, soaked and
drained
125g/5 oz oat groats, soaked and drained
350g/12 oz lean leg of beef, cubed
2 × 15ml spoons/2 tablespoons olive oil
1 medium onion, sliced
1 clove of garlic, finely chopped
1 × 5ml spoon/1 teaspoon paprika
½ × 2.5ml spoon/¼ teaspoon grated
nutmeg
1 × 15ml spoon/1 tablespoon fine
oatmeal

1 × 15ml spoon/1 tablespoon
concentrated tomato purée
450ml/¾ pint hot chicken stock
1 × 15ml spoon/1 tablespoon lemon
juice
2 × 15ml spoons/2 tablespoons chopped
parsley
salt, freshly ground pepper
4 × 15ml spoons/4 tablespoons low-fat
yoghurt
1 × 15ml spoon/1 tablespoon chopped
coriander leaves **or** parsley

Cook the chick-peas and the groats in separate pans of boiling water for 1 hour, then drain.

Fry the cubes of meat in a non-stick pan over moderate heat until browned, turning them often. Remove the meat with a slotted spoon, and discard the fat.

Heat the oil in a flameproof casserole, and cook the onion and garlic over moderate heat for 3 minutes, stirring once or twice. Stir in the paprika and nutmeg, and cook for 1 minute. Stir in the oatmeal and tomato purée, and cook for a further minute. Add the meat, then pour on the hot stock and lemon juice, stirring all the time. Heat to boiling point, then cover and simmer over low heat for 1 hour. Add the chick-peas and groats, then heat to boiling point. Cover, then simmer for a further hour. Stir in the chopped parsley, and season with salt and pepper. Swirl the yoghurt over the casserole just before serving, and sprinkle with the chopped herb. Serve hot.

POACHER'S STEW

25g/1 oz fine oatmeal
salt, freshly ground pepper
2 × 5ml spoons/2 teaspoons dried basil
1 × 2.5ml spoon/½ teaspoon ground mace
900g/2 lb rabbit pieces
40g/1½ oz sunflower margarine
350g/12 oz onions, thinly sliced
2 cloves garlic, finely chopped
350g/12 oz carrots, diced
2 stalks celery, thinly sliced
2 × 15ml spoons/2 tablespoons concentrated tomato purée

600ml/1 pint hot chicken stock
225g/8 oz tomatoes, skinned and sliced
1 × 15ml spoon/1 tablespoon lemon juice
2 × 15ml spoons/2 tablespoons jumbo oats **or** rolled porridge oats
2 × 15ml spoons/2 tablespoons chopped parsley

GARNISH

4 slices Oat Bread (page 92), cut into triangles, toasted

Put the oatmeal, salt, pepper, basil and mace into a bag, then toss the rabbit pieces in the mixture to coat them thoroughly.

Melt the margarine in a flameproof casserole, and fry the rabbit pieces over moderate heat, turning them to brown them evenly on all sides. Remove with a slotted spoon, and keep warm.

Put the onions, garlic, carrots and celery in the casserole, stir well and fry for 3 minutes, stirring occasionally. Stir in any remaining oatmeal.

Stir the tomato purée into the hot stock, then pour it slowly on to the vegetables, stirring all the time. Add the tomatoes, and heat to boiling point. Return the rabbit to the casserole, and heat again to boiling point, then cover and simmer for 1½ hours or until the rabbit is tender. Remove the rabbit with a slotted spoon, and keep warm.

Liquidize the vegetables and stock in a blender, then sieve the purée. Alternatively, rub the vegetables through a sieve or purée them in a vegetable mill. Stir the lemon juice and oats into the purée, then season to taste. Return the purée to the casserole, add the rabbit, and re-heat gently, stirring in the parsley. Garnish with the triangles of toast.

CRUNCHY SPICED VEGETABLES

SERVES 4-6

25g/1 oz sunflower margarine
1 × 15ml spoon/1 tablespoon sunflower oil
2 medium onions, sliced
2 cloves garlic, finely chopped
1 piece of fresh ginger root, peeled and finely chopped
1 × 5ml spoon/1 teaspoon ground coriander
1 × 5ml spoon/1 teaspoon curry powder
1 × 2.5ml spoon/½ teaspoon coriander seeds, lightly crushed
1 × 2.5ml spoon/½ teaspoon cardamom seeds, lightly crushed
1 medium cauliflower, cut into florets
3 medium carrots, thinly sliced
2 medium courgettes, sliced

1 green pepper, de-seeded and sliced
1 red pepper, de-seeded and sliced
225g/8 oz green beans
1 dessert apple, cored and sliced
300ml/½ pint chicken stock
4 × 15ml spoons/4 tablespoons pinhead oatmeal
salt, freshly ground pepper

GARNISH

4 × 15ml spoons/4 tablespoons jumbo oats, toasted
3 × 15ml spoons/3 tablespoons chopped almonds, toasted
1 × 15ml spoon/1 tablespoon sunflower seeds, toasted

Heat the margarine and oil in a flameproof casserole, and cook the onions, garlic and ginger over moderate heat for 3 minutes, stirring frequently. Stir in the spices, and cook for 1 minute. Add the vegetables, apple, stock and oatmeal, stir well and heat slowly to boiling point. Cover the dish and simmer for 20 minutes, stirring occasionally, until the vegetables are just tender. Season with salt and pepper. Sprinkle the oats, almonds and seeds over the vegetables, and serve hot.

Serve with cooked oat groats.

OPPOSITE *Vegetable Basket*

VEGETABLE BASKET

2 × 15ml spoons/2 tablespoons
sunflower oil
1 medium onion, sliced
4 stalks celery, thinly sliced
2 medium carrots, thinly sliced
½ small white cabbage, shredded
2 medium courgettes, sliced
1 × 2.5ml spoon/½ teaspoon cumin
seeds
1 × 15ml spoon/1 tablespoon paprika

1 × 5ml spoon/1 teaspoon dried oregano
1 × 15ml spoon/1 tablespoon
concentrated tomato purée
600ml/1 pint tomato juice
300ml/½ pint chicken stock
salt, freshly ground pepper
4 × 15ml spoons/4 tablespoons jumbo
oats **or** rolled porridge oats
150ml/¼ pint low-fat soured cream
chopped marjoram **or** parsley

Heat the oil in a flameproof casserole, and fry the onion and celery over moderate heat for 3 minutes, stirring once or twice. Add the carrots, cabbage and courgettes, and cook for 5 minutes, stirring frequently. Stir in the cumin seeds, paprika and dried oregano, and cook for 1 minute, then add the tomato purée, tomato juice and stock. Stir well and heat to boiling point. Cover the dish and simmer for 15 minutes or until the vegetables are just tender. Season with salt and pepper, then stir in the oats and all but 2 × 15ml spoons/ 2 tablespoons of the soured cream. Heat gently. Swirl the remaining soured cream over the vegetables, and scatter the top with the fresh herbs. Serve hot.

Serve this vegetable hotpot sprinkled with uncooked oat groats.

The Main Attraction

When you have added oats and oatmeal to pastry and pizza bases and to a savoury filling for poultry, fish and vegetables; tossed whole fish and fillets of meat in an oaty crumb mixture; made a colourful and tasty pilaf with oat groats; finished off a hearty casserole with a cheesy oat topping; and extended the meat content in pies, loaves and fillings with this fibre-full cereal, you will wonder what, if anything, oats cannot do.

Fine oatmeal stirred into a sauce is a soluble fibre thickening agent; medium or coarse grades – pinhead oatmeal – and rolled oats can be used in place of breadcrumbs to provide the 'bulk' in fillings; and used to extend meat they both absorb the flavour and enable you to cut down on saturated animal fat. As grilled or baked toppings, rolled oats need to be mixed with a moist vegetable – tomatoes for example – fat or cheese if they are not to burn. A Dutch hard cheese which is lowest in fat content or, better still, cottage cheese is suitable.

'If you use oats in all these ways, doesn't everything begin to taste like porridge?' a colleague asked doubtfully. Well, there's only one way to find out. Here's another chapter of recipes. The proof of the pudding. . . .

NORWICH BAKED VEGETABLES

1 small cauliflower, cut into florets
2 medium carrots, diced
1 medium parsnip, diced
salt, freshly ground pepper
100g/4 oz cooked dried haricot beans

SAUCE

25g/1 oz sunflower margarine
2 × 15ml spoons/2 tablespoons oatbran and oatgerm
1 × 5ml spoon/1 teaspoon dry English mustard

300ml/½ pint buttermilk
100g/4 oz cottage cheese
2 × 15ml spoons/2 tablespoons chopped parsley

TOPPING

50g/2 oz rolled porridge oats
50g/2 oz chopped hazelnuts
100g/4 oz cottage cheese

Steam the cauliflower, carrots and parsnip over boiling salted water until tender. Transfer them to a baking dish, then stir in the haricot beans.

To make the sauce, melt the margarine in a small pan, and stir in the oatbran and mustard until the mixture is smooth. Slowly pour on the buttermilk, stirring constantly. Heat the sauce to boiling point, and simmer for 3 minutes. Season with salt and pepper. Stir in the cottage cheese and the parsley, then pour the sauce over the vegetables.

Mix together the topping ingredients, and sprinkle them over the vegetables. Bake in a fairly hot oven, 190°C/375°F/Gas 5, for 35 minutes until the topping is brown and crisp.

VEGETABLE DECKER

2 × 15ml spoons/2 tablespoons
sunflower oil
1 large onion, sliced
2 courgettes, diced
1 aubergine, diced
4 stalks celery, thinly sliced
2 red peppers, de-seeded and chopped
100g/4 oz mushrooms, sliced
350g/12 oz tomatoes, skinned and sliced
225ml/8 fl oz chicken stock

1 × 5ml spoon/1 teaspoon dried mixed
herbs
salt, freshly ground pepper
25g/1 oz rolled porridge oats

FILLING

50g/2 oz wholewheat breadcrumbs
50g/2 oz rolled porridge oats
25g/1 oz jumbo oats
50g/2 oz Edam cheese, grated

Heat the oil in a frying pan, and fry all the vegetables over moderate heat for 2-3 minutes, stirring frequently. Pour on the stock, add the herbs, and season with salt and pepper. Heat to boiling point, then simmer, uncovered, for 5 minutes. Stir in the oats.

Mix together the filling ingredients, and layer alternately in a baking dish with the vegetables. Cover with foil or a lid, and bake in a fairly hot oven, 190°C/375°F/Gas 5, for 30 minutes. Remove the lid, and cook for a further 10 minutes to brown the topping.

SARDINE PIZZA

175g/6 oz wholewheat self-raising flour
50g/2 oz rolled porridge oats
salt, freshly ground pepper
50g/2 oz sunflower margarine
1 × 5ml spoon/1 teaspoon dried mixed
herbs
6 × 15ml spoons/6 tablespoons low-fat
yoghurt
fine oatmeal for dusting

FILLING AND TOPPING

400g/14 oz canned tomatoes
1 small onion, sliced
1 clove of garlic, crushed
1 × 5ml spoon/1 teaspoon dried mixed
herbs
1 medium courgette, diced
2 × 15ml spoons/2 tablespoons fine
oatmeal
salt, freshly ground pepper
225g/8 oz sardines in oil, drained
2 × 15ml spoons/2 tablespoons black
olives, halved and pitted
50g/2 oz Gruyère **or** Edam cheese, very
thinly sliced

Make the filling first. Put the tomatoes, onion, garlic, herbs and courgette into a small pan. Heat to boiling point, then simmer for 20 minutes. Sprinkle on the oatmeal, and quickly stir it in. Season with salt and pepper. Simmer again if necessary to reduce to a thick paste. Put to one side to cool.

Meanwhile, mix together the flour and oats, and season with salt and pepper. Rub in the margarine. Stir in the herbs, and mix to a firm dough with the yoghurt. Lightly dust a sheet of greaseproof paper with fine oatmeal. Roll out the dough and shape it to a 20cm/8 inch round, pressing up the edges.

Place the dough on a baking sheet. Spread it with the cooled tomato filling. Split the sardines in half lengthways, and remove the bones. Arrange them, cut sides down, in a wheel pattern. Arrange the olives, and cover the sardines with the cheese. Bake in a hot oven, 220°C/425°F/Gas 7, for 15-20 minutes until crisp. Serve hot.

MUSHROOM QUICHE

25g/1 oz sunflower margarine
1 small onion, finely chopped
1 clove of garlic, crushed
225g/8 oz button mushrooms, sliced
100g/4 oz cottage cheese, sieved
150ml/¼ pint low-fat soured cream
150ml/¼ pint skimmed milk
1 × 15ml spoon/1 tablespoon chopped
parsley
2 eggs

salt, freshly ground pepper

RICH OATMEAL PASTRY

75g/3 oz rolled porridge oats
75g/3 oz wholewheat self-raising flour
salt
75g/3 oz sunflower margarine
1 egg, beaten
fine oatmeal for dusting

Make the pastry first. Mix together the oats, flour and salt. Rub in the margarine, and bind the mixture to a dough with the beaten egg. Lightly dust a sheet of greaseproof paper with fine oatmeal. Roll out the dough to 6mm/¼ inch thickness, and use to line a 20cm/8 inch flan ring. Trim the edges, and prick the base with a fork.

Melt the margarine in a pan, and fry the onion and garlic over moderate heat for 3 minutes, stirring once or twice. Cool slightly.

Spread the onion and garlic over the flan base, and arrange the mushrooms on top. Beat together the cheese, soured cream, milk, parsley and eggs, and season with salt and pepper. Pour the filling over the mushrooms. Stand the flan case on a baking sheet, and bake in a fairly hot oven, 190°C/375°F/Gas 5, for 35 minutes until the filling is set. Serve hot.

GARDEN VEGETABLE FLAN

225g/8 oz small French beans
350g/12 oz broad beans (shelled weight)
2 medium carrots, thinly sliced
2 medium courgettes, thinly sliced
100g/4 oz canned sweetcorn kernels,
drained
salt, freshly ground pepper
300ml/½ pint buttermilk
2 × 5ml spoons/2 teaspoons lemon juice

2 × 15ml spoons/2 tablespoons chopped
parsley
2 eggs

OATMEAL PASTRY

50g/2 oz medium oatmeal
25g/1 oz jumbo oats
75g/3 oz wholewheat flour
salt
75g/3 oz sunflower margarine
fine oatmeal for dusting

Steam the vegetables over boiling salted water until just tender. Plunge them into cold water to prevent further cooking, then drain. Put to one side to cool.

Meanwhile, make the pastry. Mix together the oatmeal, oats, flour and salt. Rub in the margarine, and sprinkle on enough water to make a firm dough. Lightly dust a sheet of greaseproof paper with fine oatmeal. Roll out the dough to 6mm/¼ inch thickness, and use to line a 20cm/8 inch flan ring. Trim the edges, and prick the base with a fork.

Beat together the buttermilk, lemon juice, parsley and eggs, and season to taste.

Spread the cooled vegetables in the flan case. Pour on the buttermilk mixture, then stand the flan case on a baking sheet. Bake in a fairly hot oven, 190°C/375°F/Gas 5, for 35 minutes or until the filling is set. Serve warm.

OPPOSITE *Mushroom Quiche, Sardine Pizza (page 45) and Garden Vegetable Flan*

CARROT CRUMBLE

450g/1 lb cooked carrots, thinly sliced
15g/½ oz sunflower margarine
1 × 2.5ml spoon/½ teaspoon ground ginger
1 × 5ml spoon/1 teaspoon clear honey
225g/8 oz canned sweetcorn kernels, drained
1 × 15ml spoon/1 tablespoon chopped parsley
5 × 15ml spoons/5 tablespoons chicken stock
salt, freshly ground pepper

TOPPING

50g/2 oz medium oatmeal
2 × 15ml spoons/2 tablespoons sesame seeds
2 × 15ml spoons/2 tablespoons chopped hazelnuts
salt, freshly ground pepper
4 × 15ml spoons/4 tablespoons sunflower oil

Mix the carrots with the margarine, ginger, honey, sweetcorn, parsley and chicken stock, then season with salt and pepper. Pour the vegetable mixture into a baking dish.

Mix together the topping ingredients, and spread this over the vegetables. Bake in a fairly hot oven, 190°C/375°F/Gas 5, for 20 minutes until the topping is crisp and brown. Serve hot.

Note A green salad is a specially good contrast and complement to this dish.

CABBAGE ROLLS

12 large, tender cabbage leaves, stalks removed
salt, freshly ground pepper
1 × 15ml spoon/1 tablespoon concentrated tomato purée
300ml/½ pint hot chicken stock

FILLING

25g/1 oz sunflower margarine
1 × 15ml spoon/1 tablespoon sunflower oil

1 medium onion, chopped
2 stalks tender celery, finely chopped
175g/6 oz chopped hazelnuts
50g/2 oz rolled porridge oats
50g/2 oz dried apricot pieces, soaked and drained
3 × 15ml spoons/3 tablespoons chopped parsley
1 × 5ml spoon/1 teaspoon dried oregano
salt, freshly ground pepper
a pinch of grated nutmeg
2 eggs, beaten

Cook the cabbage leaves in boiling salted water for 3 minutes, then drain and pat dry with kitchen paper.

To make the filling, heat the margarine and oil in a pan, and fry the onion and celery over moderate heat for 3 minutes, stirring once or twice. Stir in the nuts and oats, and remove from the heat. Stir in the apricots and herbs, and season the mixture with salt, pepper and nutmeg. Beat in the eggs.

Place the cabbage leaves flat, with the stalk side towards you. Place a spoonful of the mixture in the centre of each leaf. Fold over the stalk end, then each of the two sides to enclose the filling. Make neat parcels. Place the parcels, join sides down, in a frying pan.

Mix the tomato purée with the hot stock, and season with salt and pepper. Pour it over the leaves, cover the pan, heat to boiling point, then simmer for 30 minutes. Serve hot.

Note Potatoes steamed in their skins go well with this dish.

COURGETTE CRISP

2 × 15ml spoons/2 tablespoons
sunflower oil
450g/1 lb courgettes, cut into 6mm/
¼ inch slices
1 small aubergine, thinly sliced
2 cloves garlic, crushed
225g/8 oz tomatoes, skinned and sliced
1 × 5ml spoon/1 teaspoon dried
marjoram
2 × 15ml spoons/2 tablespoons chopped
parsley
salt, freshly ground pepper

SAUCE AND TOPPING

225g/8 oz cottage cheese, sieved
2 eggs
300ml/½ pint low-fat yoghurt
salt, freshly ground pepper
a pinch of grated nutmeg
50g/2 oz chopped walnuts
50g/2 oz jumbo oats

Heat a little of the oil in a frying pan, and fry the courgette and aubergine slices in batches to brown them lightly, greasing the pan with a little more oil each time.

Transfer the vegetables to a baking dish. Add the garlic, and fry over moderate heat for 1 minute. Add the tomato slices and herbs, and cook for 2-3 minutes. Spread the tomatoes over the dish, and season with salt and pepper.

To make the sauce, beat together half the cheese, the eggs and yoghurt, and season with salt, pepper and nutmeg. Pour the sauce over the dish.

Mix the walnuts and oats with the remaining cheese, and sprinkle this over the sauce. Stand the dish on a baking tray, and bake in a fairly hot oven, 190°C/375°F/Gas 5, for 30-35 minutes until the topping is crisp and brown. Serve hot.

BEAN PEPPERS

4 large green **or** red peppers
150ml/¼ pint chicken stock

FILLING

175g/6 oz cooked dried beans, eg haricot
or flageolet
1 small onion, finely chopped
2 cloves garlic, crushed
50g/2 oz rolled porridge oats

50g/2 oz chopped walnuts
50g/2 oz mushrooms, chopped
2 large tomatoes, skinned and chopped
salt, freshly ground pepper
1 × 5ml spoon/1 teaspoon dried savory
1 × 15ml spoon/1 tablespoon chopped
parsley
25g/1 oz sunflower margarine, melted
50g/2 oz cottage cheese

Cut a thin slice from the top of each of the peppers. Remove the seeds and core. Blanch the peppers and tops in boiling water for 5 minutes. Drain them and stand the peppers upside-down to dry.

To make the filling, mix together the beans, onion, garlic, oats, walnuts, mushrooms and tomatoes. Season the mixture with salt, pepper and the herbs, then pour on the margarine, and mix well.

Stand the peppers upright in a greased baking dish that just fits them. Pack the filling into the peppers, mounding it to a dome on top. Press the cottage cheese on to the filling. Pour the stock around the peppers, then cook in a moderate oven, 180°C/350°F/Gas 4, for 30 minutes until the filling is bubbling. Serve hot.

SPICED LENTIL PILAF

2 × 15ml spoons/2 tablespoons
sunflower oil
2 medium onions, chopped
2 cloves garlic, finely chopped
1 green pepper, de-seeded and chopped
1 red pepper, de-seeded and chopped
1 × 5ml spoon/1 teaspoon ground cumin
1 × 5ml spoon/1 teaspoon curry powder
1 × 2.5ml spoon/½ teaspoon ground
turmeric
175g/6 oz oat groats, soaked and drained
50g/2 oz rolled porridge oats
900ml/1½ pints chicken stock (approx)
225g/8 oz brown lentils, washed and
drained
4 × 15ml spoons/4 tablespoons seedless
raisins
4 × 15ml spoons/4 tablespoons cashew
nuts

2 × 15ml spoons/2 tablespoons chopped
coriander leaves **or** parsley
salt, freshly ground pepper

SAUCE

150ml/¼ pint low-fat yoghurt
2 × 15ml spoons/2 tablespoons chopped
coriander leaves **or** parsley
1 × 5ml spoon/1 teaspoon lemon juice
paprika

GARNISH

banana slices
lemon juice
3 × 15ml spoons/3 tablespoons
shredded coconut

Heat the oil in a flameproof casserole, and fry the onions and garlic over moderate heat for 2 minutes. Stir in the green and red peppers, and cook for a further 2 minutes. Stir in the spices, groats and rolled oats, and cook for 1 minute. Pour on the stock. Heat to boiling point, then simmer for 30 minutes. Add the lentils. Heat to boiling point, then simmer for 45 minutes. Add more stock or water if the dish begins to dry out. Stir in the raisins, nuts and herb, and season with salt and pepper. Simmer for 2-3 minutes.

Meanwhile, stir together the yoghurt, coriander and lemon juice for the sauce. Sprinkle with the paprika.

Garnish the pilaf with the banana slices tossed in lemon juice, and sprinkle the coconut on top. Serve the sauce separately.

NUT PILAF

225g/8 oz oat groats, soaked and drained
2 × 15ml spoons/2 tablespoons
sunflower oil
1 medium onion, thinly sliced
1 clove of garlic, crushed
4 stalks celery, thinly sliced
1 red pepper, de-seeded and chopped
1 green pepper, de-seeded and chopped

75g/3 oz walnuts, chopped
225g/8 oz button mushrooms, sliced
4 × 15ml spoons/4 tablespoons white
wine
salt, freshly ground pepper
2 × 5ml spoons/2 teaspoons chopped
thyme

Cook the groats in boiling water for 1¼ hours, then drain thoroughly and rinse under cold, running water.

Heat the oil in a pan, and cook the onion and garlic over moderate heat for 3 minutes, stirring once or twice. Add the celery, red and green peppers, the nuts, mushrooms and groats. Stir well, then cook for 2 minutes, stirring frequently. Pour on the wine, and season with salt and pepper. Simmer for 5 minutes, then stir in the thyme. Serve hot.

Serve with a green salad.

Spiced Lentil Pilaf

GINGER AND PEANUT LOAF

2 × 15ml spoons/2 tablespoons sunflower oil
1 large onion, chopped
1 clove of garlic, finely chopped
1 red pepper, de-seeded and chopped
1 piece of root ginger, peeled, chopped and crushed
100g/4 oz mushrooms, chopped
25g/1 oz fine oatmeal
175g/6 oz unsalted peanuts, ground
1 × 15ml spoon/1 tablespoon concentrated tomato purée
4 tomatoes, skinned and chopped

75g/3 oz rolled porridge oats
1 × 15ml spoon/1 tablespoon clear honey
1 × 15ml spoon/1 tablespoon soy sauce
3 × 15ml spoons/3 tablespoons medium sherry
2 × 15ml spoons/2 tablespoons orange juice
1 × 5ml spoon/1 teaspoon grated orange rind
1 egg, beaten
6-8 young spinach leaves, without stalks (optional)

Heat the oil in a pan, and fry the onion, garlic, pepper and ginger over moderate heat for 3 minutes, stirring frequently. Stir in the mushrooms, and cook over low heat for 5 minutes. Stir in the oatmeal, and cook for 1 minute. Remove the pan from the heat, then stir in the peanuts, tomato purée, tomatoes and oats. Mix together the honey, soy sauce, sherry, orange juice and rind and the egg. Pour this on to the nut mixture, and beat until smooth.

Line a greased 450g/1 lb loaf tin with the spinach leaves, if used. Fill the tin with the nut mixture, and cover with foil. Stand the tin in a roasting pan half filled with warm water, and bake in a fairly hot oven, 190°C/375°F/Gas 5, for 50 minutes. Leave in the tin for 5 minutes, then turn out. Serve hot, with vegetables, or cold, with salad.

SEAFOOD COURGETTES

225g/8 oz fillet of cod **or** haddock
200ml/7 fl oz skimmed milk
1 medium onion, halved
1 clove
1 bay leaf
4 × 15ml spoons/4 tablespoons rolled porridge oats
2 × 15ml spoons/2 tablespoons jumbo oats

4 large courgettes
1 × 15ml spoon/1 tablespoon sunflower oil
125g/5 oz cottage cheese
1 egg
salt, freshly ground pepper
2 × 15ml spoons/2 tablespoons chopped parsley
50g/2 oz Edam cheese, grated

Poach the fish for 10 minutes in the milk with half the onion, the clove and bay leaf. Lift out the fish and skin it. Remove any bones, and flake the fish. Discard the onion, clove and bay leaf. Stir the oats into the milk, and heat to boiling point, stirring constantly. Remove from the heat.

Trim and halve the courgettes and scoop out the flesh, taking care not to pierce the skins. Chop the flesh.

Chop the remaining onion half. Heat the oil in a pan, and fry the onion and courgette flesh over moderate heat for 3 minutes, stirring frequently.

Beat the courgette mixture, the flaked fish, cottage cheese and egg into the oats, then season with salt and pepper, and stir in the parsley.

Place the courgette halves in a shallow baking dish. Pack the mixture into the shells, and shape into neat mounds. Sprinkle with the grated cheese. Cook in a fairly hot oven, 200°C/400°F/Gas 6, for 30 minutes until bubbling. Serve hot.

Note New potatoes and a green vegetable such as calabrese complete a light meal. Alternatively, you can serve the courgettes with a green salad and tomatoes.

HOT PEPPER FISH

4 haddock fillets (175g/6 oz each approx), skinned and boned
400g/14 oz canned tomatoes
1 red pepper, de-seeded and sliced
1 green pepper, de-seeded and sliced
1 large onion, thinly sliced
1 × 5ml spoon/1 teaspoon dried tarragon
1 × 2.5ml spoon/½ teaspoon Tabasco sauce
salt, freshly ground pepper

TOPPING

50g/2 oz rolled porridge oats
50g/2 oz wholewheat flour
salt, freshly ground pepper
100g/4 oz cottage cheese
25g/1 oz Gruyère **or** Edam cheese, grated

Place the fish in a greased baking dish.

Put the canned tomatoes into a pan, and add the sliced peppers, onion, tarragon and Tabasco sauce. Season with salt and pepper. Heat to boiling point, then simmer for 15 minutes until the mixture thickens. Remove from the heat.

Mix together the ingredients for the topping.

Pour the tomato sauce over the fish, and spread the topping evenly over it. Place the dish on a baking sheet, and bake in a fairly hot oven, 190°C/375°F/Gas 5, for 15 minutes until bubbling.

SPECKLED TROUT

4 trout, scaled, cleaned, washed and dried
3 × 15ml spoons/3 tablespoons fine oatmeal
1 × 5ml spoon/1 teaspoon dried thyme
25g/1 oz sunflower margarine

FILLING AND COATING

25g/1 oz sunflower margarine
1 small onion, finely chopped
2 bacon rashers, without rinds, chopped
2 × 15ml spoons/2 tablespoons medium oatmeal
100g/4 oz canned sweetcorn kernels, drained
2 × 15ml spoons/2 tablespoons chopped parsley
2 × 15ml spoons/2 tablespoons lemon juice
2 × 5ml spoons/2 teaspoons grated lemon rind
salt, freshly ground pepper

GARNISH

lemon wedges

Prepare the filling first. Melt the margarine in a pan, and fry the onion and bacon over moderate heat for 3 minutes, stirring once or twice. Stir in the medium oatmeal, sweetcorn, parsley, lemon juice and half the lemon rind. Season with salt and pepper, then remove from the heat. Leave to cool.

Pack the filling into the fish cavities. Mix the remaining lemon rind with the fine oatmeal and dried thyme. Toss the fish in this mixture to coat it thoroughly on all sides.

Line a grill pan with foil. Melt the remaining margarine in a pan. Brush the foil with the margarine, and place the fish on it side by side. Drizzle the rest of the margarine over the fish. Grill under moderate heat for 5-6 minutes on each side. Serve at once, garnished with the lemon wedges.

Note Tomato salad garnished with thinly sliced onion rings is a good accompaniment.

COD CUTLETS WITH OLIVES

4 cod cutlets (175g/6 oz each approx), boned
50g/2 oz Edam cheese, grated

FILLING

25g/1 oz sunflower margarine
1 small onion, chopped
½ green pepper, de-seeded and chopped
2 × 15ml spoons/2 tablespoons medium oatmeal
1 × 15ml spoon/1 tablespoon jumbo oats
1 × 15ml/1 tablespoon chopped parsley
1 × 5ml spoon/1 teaspoon grated orange rind
2 × 15ml spoons/2 tablespoons orange juice
3 × 15ml spoons/3 tablespoons black olives, stoned and chopped
freshly ground pepper

Make the filling first. Melt the margarine in a pan, and fry the onion and pepper over moderate heat for 3 minutes, stirring frequently. Remove from the heat and stir in the oatmeal, oats, parsley, orange rind, orange juice and olives. Season with pepper.

Place the cod cutlets in a greased shallow baking dish. Pack the filling into the bone cavity, and sprinkle with the cheese. Bake in a moderate oven, 180°C/350°F/Gas 4, for 20 minutes until bubbling. Serve hot.

Note New potatoes, and sweetcorn tossed in yoghurt and chopped parsley complete a nutritious meal.

OPPOSITE *Hake Stir-fry*

HAKE STIR-FRY

675g/1½ lb hake, skinned, filleted and cut into 2.5cm/1 inch slices
4 × 15ml spoons/4 tablespoons orange juice
1 × 5ml spoon/1 teaspoon grated orange rind
3 × 15ml spoons/3 tablespoons fine oatmeal
salt, freshly ground pepper
a pinch of ground mace
1 × 5ml spoon/1 teaspoon fennel seed
2 × 15ml spoons/2 tablespoons sunflower oil

1 medium onion, sliced
1 clove of garlic, finely chopped
1 red pepper, de-seeded and sliced
1 green pepper, de-seeded and sliced
3 stalks celery, thinly sliced
4 × 15ml spoons/4 tablespoons cashew nuts
2 × 15ml spoons/2 tablespoons jumbo oats
1 × 15ml spoon/1 tablespoon chopped parsley
strips of orange rind

Toss the fish in the orange juice and orange rind. Cover and leave to marinate for at least 1 hour. Drain the fish. Put the oatmeal, salt, pepper, mace and fennel seed into a bag, then toss the fish in the mixture to coat it thoroughly.

Heat the oil in a large frying pan, and stir-fry the fish over moderate heat for 5 minutes, then remove from the pan.

Fry the onion, garlic, peppers and celery in the pan for 4-5 minutes, stirring frequently. Return the fish to the pan, stir in the nuts, oats and parsley, and cook for 2 minutes. Serve hot, garnished with the orange rind.

Note Low-fat yoghurt swirled over the fish is a good 'extra'.

LONELY SHEPHERD

350g/12 oz lean lamb, minced
1 large onion, chopped
4 stalks celery, thinly sliced
75g/3 oz rolled porridge oats
100g/4 oz mushrooms, sliced
175g/6 oz canned pimentos, drained and chopped
400g/14 oz canned tomatoes
150ml/¼ pint tomato juice
1 × 15ml spoon/1 tablespoon Worcestershire sauce
1 × 15ml spoon/1 tablespoon concentrated tomato purée

1 × 5ml spoon/1 teaspoon mixed dried herbs
salt, freshly ground pepper

TOPPING

450g/1 lb potatoes, peeled
salt, freshly ground pepper
25g/1 oz sunflower margarine
3 × 15ml spoons/3 tablespoons skimmed milk
1 large carrot, grated
50g/2 oz Wensleydale cheese, crumbled

Fry the lamb in a non-stick pan over moderate heat, stirring frequently, to melt the fat. Lift out the meat with a slotted spoon. Discard all but 2 × 5ml spoons/2 teaspoons of the fat.

Cook the onion and celery in the pan for 3 minutes, stirring frequently. Add the meat and all the remaining ingredients, seasoning the mixture well with salt and pepper. Turn the mixture into a baking dish.

To make the topping, cook the potatoes in boiling, salted water until tender, then drain and mash them with the margarine and milk. Beat in the grated carrot and cheese, and season with salt and pepper.

Spread the potato topping over the meat mixture, and level the surface. Stand the dish on a baking tray, and bake in a fairly hot oven, 190°C/375°F/Gas 5, for 35-40 minutes until the topping is well browned. Serve hot.

SPINACH AND VEAL ROLLS

4 veal escalopes, flattened
25g/1 oz sunflower oil
1 × 15ml spoon/1 tablespoon
wholewheat flour
150ml/¼ pint dry white wine
salt, freshly ground pepper
4 × 15ml spoons/4 tablespoons
Greek-style yoghurt
sprigs parsley

FILLING

1 × 15ml spoon/1 tablespoon sunflower
oil

1 small onion, chopped
1 clove of garlic, crushed
100g/4 oz cooked spinach, well drained
and chopped
40g/1½ oz chopped walnuts
3 × 15ml spoons/3 tablespoons jumbo
oats
2 × 15ml spoons/2 tablespoons grated
Parmesan cheese
salt, freshly ground pepper
a pinch of grated nutmeg

Make the filling first. Heat the oil in a pan, and cook the onion and garlic over moderate heat for 3 minutes, stirring once or twice. Put the spinach into a bowl, then beat in the onion mixture, the walnuts, oats and the cheese. Season with salt, pepper and nutmeg.

Divide the filling between the escalopes. Roll up the meat to enclose the filling, and tie the rolls with string.

Heat the remaining oil in a frying pan, and fry the rolls over moderate heat, turning them frequently, until evenly browned. Remove the meat from the pan.

Stir the flour into the pan, and pour on the wine, stirring constantly. Heat to boiling point, then season with salt and pepper. Return the veal rolls to the pan, cover and simmer for 15 minutes, then transfer the meat to a heated serving dish.

Boil the sauce for 2 minutes until reduced, then stir in the yoghurt. Season to taste, then pour a little of the sauce over the meat, and garnish with the parsley. Serve the remaining sauce separately.

CHICKEN AND VEGETABLE LOAF

SERVES 6-8

25g/1 oz sunflower margarine
1 medium onion, quartered
1 clove of garlic
2 stalks celery, thinly sliced
2 courgettes, sliced
1 medium carrot, diced
550g/1¼ lb raw chicken, minced
150ml/¼ pint tomato juice
1 × 5ml spoon/1 teaspoon
Worcestershire sauce

50g/2 oz rolled porridge oats
25g/1 oz jumbo oats
salt, freshly ground pepper
1 × 5ml spoon/1 teaspoon dried oregano
2 × 15ml spoons/2 tablespoons chopped
parsley
1 egg, beaten
2 hard-boiled eggs, sliced

Melt the margarine in a frying pan, and fry the onion, garlic, celery, courgettes and carrot over moderate heat for 2-3 minutes, stirring frequently. Stir in the chicken, and cook for 3 minutes, stirring constantly. Remove the pan from the heat and stir in the tomato juice, Worcestershire sauce and oats. Season with salt and pepper, then stir in the herbs. Beat in the egg, and beat the mixture well.

Press half the mixture into a greased 900g/2 lb loaf tin, and arrange the egg slices on top. Cover with the remaining mixture. Cover the tin with foil, and stand it in a roasting pan half filled with warm water. Cook in a moderate oven, 180°C/350°F/Gas 4, for 1¼ hours. Leave to cool slightly, then pour off any liquid. Turn out the loaf on to a heated serving dish, and serve hot or cold.

CRISPY CHICKEN

2 × 15ml spoons/2 tablespoons fine
oatmeal
1 × 15ml spoon/1 tablespoon oatbran
and oatgerm (optional)
salt, freshly ground pepper
4 slices boneless chicken breast
(125-175g/5-6 oz each approx)
6 × 15ml spoons/6 tablespoons jumbo
oats
3 × 15ml spoons/3 tablespoons chopped
hazelnuts
1 × 2.5ml spoon/½ teaspoon ground
coriander

1 × 2.5ml spoon/½ teaspoon coriander
seeds, crushed
1 × 5ml spoon/1 teaspoon dried thyme
1 egg, beaten

SAUCE

225ml/8 fl oz low-fat yoghurt
50g/2 oz hazelnuts, chopped
2 × 15ml spoons/2 tablespoons sweet
sherry
1 × 5ml spoon/1 teaspoon chopped
parsley

Put the oatmeal, oatbran, salt and pepper into a bag, then toss the chicken slices in the mixture to coat them thoroughly. Mix together the jumbo oats, hazelnuts, ground coriander seeds and thyme. Dip the chicken first in the beaten egg and then in the oats mixture.

Fry the chicken in a non-stick pan over moderate heat for 8-10 minutes on each side. Serve hot.

Mix together the ingredients for the sauce, and use a little to garnish the chicken. Serve the rest separately.

Serve with a green vegetable and new potatoes steamed in their jackets.

OPPOSITE *Crispy Chicken*

CHICKEN MOUSSAKA

3 × 15ml spoons/3 tablespoons
sunflower oil
2 medium aubergines, thinly sliced
1 medium onion, chopped
1 clove of garlic, crushed
350g/12 oz raw chicken, minced
4 × 15ml spoons/4 tablespoons rolled
porridge oats
2 × 15ml spoons/2 tablespoons chopped
parsley
2 × 15ml spoons/2 tablespoons
concentrated tomato purée

150ml/¼ pint chicken stock
salt, freshly ground pepper
350g/12 oz tomatoes, skinned and sliced

TOPPING

300ml/½ pint low-fat yoghurt
1 egg
125g/5 oz cottage cheese
50g/2 oz Edam cheese, grated
salt, freshly ground pepper

Heat the oil in a frying pan, and fry the aubergine slices over moderate heat, turning once, to brown evenly on both sides. Remove from the pan.

Put the onion, garlic and chicken in the pan, and fry for 1 minute. Stir in the oats and parsley. Mix together the tomato purée and stock, pour into the pan, season with salt and pepper, and simmer until the liquid has been absorbed but the mixture is still moist.

Arrange the aubergines in a baking dish. Cover them with the chicken mixture, and arrange the sliced tomatoes on top.

Beat together the topping ingredients, then pour this over the tomatoes. Stand the dish on a baking sheet, and cook in a fairly hot oven, 190°C/375°F/Gas 5, for 45 minutes until bubbling. Serve hot or cold.

CHICKEN AUBERGINES

2 large aubergines
salt, freshly ground pepper
2 × 15ml spoons/2 tablespoons
sunflower oil
1 large onion, chopped
1 clove of garlic, crushed
2 × 15ml spoons/2 tablespoons
concentrated tomato purée
350g/12 oz cooked chicken, chopped

125ml/4 fl oz white wine
6 × 15ml spoons/6 tablespoons rolled
porridge oats
2 × 15ml spoons/2 tablespoons chopped
parsley
2 × 15ml spoons/2 tablespoons sultanas
4 × 15ml spoons/4 tablespoons grated
cheese

Slice the aubergines in half lengthways and criss-cross the flesh with deep cuts. Sprinkle with salt, and put to one side for at least 30 minutes to draw out the bitter juices.

Meanwhile, heat the oil in a pan, and fry the onion and garlic over moderate heat for 3 minutes, stirring once or twice. Stir in the tomato purée and chicken, then pour on the wine, stirring all the time. Season with salt and pepper, and stir in 2 × 15ml spoons/ 2 tablespoons of the oats. Simmer for 5 minutes until the mixture has formed a thick paste. Stir in the parsley, and remove from the heat.

Press the aubergines between your thumb and fingers to extract the moisture. Rinse them in cold water, then pat dry. Spread the chicken mixture over the vegetables. Mix the remaining oats with the sultanas and cheese, and sprinkle this over the chicken. Press the topping down firmly. Place the aubergine halves in a baking dish, and cook in a fairly hot oven, 190°C/375°F/Gas 5, for 50 minutes until bubbling. Serve hot.

Serve with brown rice and a green salad.

CHICKEN WITH WATERCRESS STUFFING

SERVES 4-6

1.45kg/3¼ lb chicken
1 × 15ml spoon/1 tablespoon lemon juice
salt, freshly ground pepper
300ml/½ pint chicken stock (made from chicken giblets)
2 × 15ml spoons/2 tablespoons orange juice
1 × 5ml spoon/1 teaspoon grated orange rind

STUFFING

1 bunch of watercress, trimmed and chopped (reserve a few sprigs to garnish)
4 spring onions, finely chopped
1 stalk of tender celery, finely chopped
2 × 15ml spoons/2 tablespoons chopped parsley
50g/2 oz rolled porridge oats
3 × 15ml spoons/3 tablespoons orange juice
2 × 5ml spoons/2 teaspoons grated orange zest
a pinch of ground ginger
50g/2 oz seedless raisins
salt, freshly ground pepper
4 × 15ml spoons/4 tablespoons low-fat yoghurt
1 egg, beaten

Mix together the ingredients for the stuffing, binding them with the egg.

Pack the stuffing into the chicken, and close the vents with skewers. Rub the skin all over with lemon juice, and season with black pepper. Place the chicken on a rack in a roasting pan. Cover with foil, and cook in a fairly hot oven, 190°C/375°F/Gas 5, for 1¼ hours. Remove the foil, and cook for a further 15 minutes. Transfer to a heated serving dish.

Pour off and discard the fat in the pan. Pour in the chicken stock and orange juice. Add the orange rind, and season with salt and pepper. Stir well, then heat the sauce to boiling point and boil for 3 minutes. Skim off any fat from the surface. Serve the sauce separately.

PHEASANT WITH OATMEAL STUFFING

SERVES 4-6

2 pheasants
25g/1 oz sunflower margarine, melted
2 × 15ml spoons/2 tablespoons fine oatmeal

STUFFING

100g/4 oz medium oatmeal
1 small onion, chopped
4 × 15ml spoons/4 tablespoons chopped parsley
40g/1½ oz sunflower margarine, melted
a pinch of grated nutmeg
salt, freshly ground pepper

Prepare the stuffing first. Mix together the oatmeal, onion, parsley, margarine, nutmeg and seasoning, and pack the stuffing into the birds.

Place the pheasants in a roasting pan. Pour the melted margarine over them, and cover with foil. Cook in a fairly hot oven, 200°C/400°F/Gas 6, for 40 minutes. Remove the foil and rub the oatmeal over the skin of the birds. Cook, uncovered, for a further 10 minutes to crispen the skin.

CANNELLONI ROLLS

8 large wholewheat cannelloni tubes
1 medium onion
1 red pepper
salt, freshly ground pepper
175g/6 oz low-fat curd cheese
100g/4 oz cooked chicken, chopped
1 × 15ml spoon/1 tablespoon concentrated tomato purée
2 × 15ml spoons/2 tablespoons chopped parsley

8 stuffed green olives, chopped
50g/2 oz chopped walnuts
5 × 15ml spoons/5 tablespoons rolled porridge oats
a pinch of Cayenne pepper
300ml/½ pint low-fat yoghurt
1 × 15ml spoon/1 tablespoon lemon juice
50g/2 oz Parmesan cheese, grated

Cook the cannelloni tubes, the onion and the pepper in boiling salted water for 4 minutes. Drain into a colander, rinse under cold water, then drain again. Pat the pasta dry with kitchen paper. Finely chop the onion. De-seed and chop the pepper.

Beat the curd cheese until smooth. Beat in the chopped onion and pepper, the chicken, 2 × 5ml spoons/2 teaspoons of the tomato purée, the parsley, olives, walnuts and 3 × 15ml spoons/3 tablespoons of the oats. Season with salt, pepper and Cayenne pepper. Spoon the filling into the pasta tubes, packing it in tightly. Arrange the pasta in a greased, shallow baking dish.

Mix together the yoghurt, lemon juice and remaining tomato purée, and season with salt and pepper. Pour this over the pasta, mix together the cheese and remaining oats, and sprinkle over the pasta. Bake in a fairly hot oven, 190°C/375°F/Gas 5, for 35 minutes until browned and bubbling. Serve hot.

Note A green salad is a cool contrast to this creamy dish. If you prefer a hot vegetable, leaf spinach is a good choice.

MARROW BOAT

1 medium marrow, peeled

FILLING AND SAUCE

1 × 15ml spoon/1 tablespoon sunflower oil
1 medium onion, chopped
350g/12 oz raw chicken, minced
100g/4 oz cooked oat groats
100g/4 oz mushrooms, chopped

1 × 15ml spoon/1 tablespoon concentrated tomato purée
2 × 5ml spoons/2 teaspoons dried mixed herbs
6 stuffed olives, chopped
a pinch of grated nutmeg
salt, freshly ground pepper
2 × 5ml spoons/2 teaspoons lemon juice
400g/14 oz canned tomatoes, chopped

Cut a slice from each end of the marrow. Use a vegetable ball scoop and, working from each end, scoop out the seeds and fibres to leave a clear channel throughout.

To make the filling, heat the oil in a pan, and cook the onion over moderate heat for 3 minutes, stirring frequently. Stir in the chicken, groats and mushrooms, and cook for 3 minutes. Stir in the tomato purée, half the herbs and the olives, and season with the nutmeg and salt and pepper. Cook for 1 minute, then add half the lemon juice. Leave to cool slightly.

Pack the filling into the marrow. Stir the remaining herbs and lemon juice into the tomatoes, and season well with salt and pepper. Pour into a baking dish, place the marrow on top, and cover the dish with foil. Cook in a fairly hot oven, 190°C/375°F/Gas 5, for 1½ hours or until the marrow is tender.

Note You can cook jacket potatoes in the oven for part of the time, and serve them topped with cottage cheese.

The Supporting Role

Creamy fennel with a crispy cheese topping; melt-in-the-mouth artichoke 'boats' filled with green pea purée; golden brown pyramids of piped potato; baked onions brimful with a vegetable and nut filling; a salad ring with a spicy, curried dressing; stir-fried sprouted grains with spring vegetables: whatever – apart from being vegetable-based – can all these dishes have in common? The answer, of course, is oats; but the ways in which the cereal is used are many and various.

Additionally, oat groats may be cooked and served 'plain', as is brown rice, or transformed into a colourful risotto with the addition of diced vegetables, meat, seafood and herbs. In much the same way, cooked oat groats tossed with salad, dried fruits and vegetables, or just with herbs, and served cold make a substantial salad. And for good measure, rolled oats and pinhead oatmeal make a crunchy contribution to salad dressings.

You can try your hand at indoor gardening – as children love to do – and start the oat groats along the way to germination. After only four or five days the result is a jar of crisp and crunchy shoots, like Chinese beansprouts, highly nutritious and, with their slightly spicy flavour, surprisingly delicious.

Rolled oats and oatmeal can be used to good effect with vegetable purées, thickening any mixture that is too 'slack' to hold its shape for piping. The cereals are invaluable, too, for absorbing any excess moisture in, for example, mashed swede, which is notorious for its habit of weeping, no matter how carefully you drain it.

Add on all the crispy toppings, cheesy sauces and tasty fillings for vegetable cases, and you have to give oats full marks for the important supporting role they play, as accompaniments to the star turn, or, if you like, the star turn itself.

LEEKS IN WHITE WINE

1 × 15ml spoon/1 tablespoon olive oil
4 × 15ml spoons/4 tablespoons white wine
8 small leeks, sliced
salt, freshly ground pepper

TOPPING

4 × 15ml spoons/4 tablespoons rolled porridge oats, toasted
2 × 15ml spoons/2 tablespoons chopped walnuts
2 × 15ml spoons/2 tablespoons chopped parsley

Heat the oil and wine in a pan to boiling point. Add the leeks, and season with salt and pepper. Simmer for about 3 minutes until the leeks are only just tender.

Mix together the ingredients for the topping, and sprinkle over the cooked leeks. Serve at once.

POTATO PYRAMIDS

SERVES 6

450g/1 lb potatoes, peeled
salt, freshly ground pepper
25g/1 oz sunflower margarine
2 × 15ml spoons/2 tablespoons low-fat yoghurt
a pinch of ground turmeric
1 egg, beaten
6 × 15ml spoons/6 tablespoons rolled porridge oats

Cook the potatoes in boiling salted water until tender, then drain them, reserving the liquid. Mash them with 2 × 15ml spoons/2 tablespoons of the reserved liquid, the margarine and yoghurt. Season with salt, pepper and turmeric, then beat in the egg, and stir in the oats. Beat the mixture well until firm and smooth.

Spoon the potato mixture into a strong piping bag with a large, plain nozzle. Pipe a 6.25cm/2½ inch circle of potato on a greased baking sheet, and, piping in spiral fashion, build it up to a pyramid shape. Continue making pyramids with the remaining mixture. Cook in a fairly hot oven, 190°C/375°F/Gas 5, for 15 minutes or until the tips are well browned. Serve at once.

Note The potato mixture can be left to cool, then re-heated just before serving.

HIGHLAND POTATOES

4 large baking potatoes, scrubbed
25g/1 oz sunflower margarine
1 small onion, chopped
100g/4 oz button mushrooms, sliced
3 × 15ml spoons/3 tablespoons jumbo oats
4 × 15ml spoons/4 tablespoons skimmed milk
2 eggs, separated
salt, freshly ground pepper
2 × 15ml spoons/2 tablespoons chopped parsley

Prick the potatoes all over with a fork to prevent the skins from bursting. Bake them in a fairly hot oven, 190°C/375°F/Gas 5, for 1¼ hours or until soft.

Meanwhile, melt the margarine in a pan, and cook the onion for 3-4 minutes. Add the mushrooms, and cook for a further 2 minutes. Stir in the oats, then remove the pan from the heat.

Halve the potatoes lengthways. Scoop out the centres, taking care not to break the skins. Mash the potato and beat in the milk and egg yolks. Stir in the oat mixture, and season with salt and pepper. Whisk the egg whites until stiff, then fold them into the mixture. Stir in the chopped parsley.

Fill the potato shells with the mixture, then place them on a baking tray, and return to the oven. Bake in a fairly hot oven, 190°C/375°F/Gas 5, for 15 minutes until bubbling. Serve hot.

OATY POTATOES

657g/1½ lb small new potatoes
salt
1 egg
2 × 15ml spoons/2 tablespoons skimmed milk
fine oatmeal for dusting
12 × 15ml spoons/12 tablespoons jumbo oats (approx)
oil for brushing

GARNISH

sprigs parsley

Cook the potatoes in boiling salted water until just tender, then drain and leave to cool.

Beat together the egg and milk. Toss the potatoes first in the fine oatmeal to coat them, and then in the egg and milk. Lift them out, draining off any excess egg, then roll in half the jumbo oats to coat them completely. Use the remaining oats to roll the potatoes a second time.

Brush a non-stick pan with oil, and heat it, then cook the potatoes over moderate heat for 4-5 minutes, turning them frequently until brown on all sides. Garnish with sprigs of parsley. Serve at once.

OAT CROQUETTES

450g/1 lb potatoes, peeled
salt, freshly ground pepper
15g/1½ oz sunflower margarine
2-4 × 15ml spoons/2-4 tablespoons skimmed milk
4 × 15ml spoons/4 tablespoons low-fat yoghurt
1 × 5ml spoon/1 teaspoon grated orange rind
40g/1½ oz rolled porridge oats
oil for brushing

COATING

1 egg
2 × 15ml spoons/2 tablespoons skimmed milk
40g/1½ oz fine oatmeal
40g/1½ oz pinhead oatmeal

Cook the potatoes in boiling salted water until tender, then drain and mash them. Beat in the margarine, milk, yoghurt and orange rind, then stir in the oats, and season with salt and pepper. Divide the mixture into 12 portions, and shape each one into a sausage shape.

Beat together the egg and milk. Toss the croquettes first in the fine oatmeal to coat them thoroughly, and then in the egg and milk to cover them on all sides. Lift them out, draining off any excess, then toss in the pinhead oatmeal, and press it well into the surface. Leave until firm.

Brush a frying pan with oil, and fry the croquettes over moderate heat for about 6 minutes, turning frequently with a wooden spoon to brown them evenly on all sides. Serve hot.

OPPOSITE *Oaty Potatoes* and *Oat Croquettes*

BAKED SWEDES

675g/1½ lb swedes, peeled and cubed
salt, freshly ground pepper
2 × 15ml spoons/2 tablespoons rolled
porridge oats
6 × 15ml spoons/6 tablespoons low-fat
yoghurt
a pinch of grated nutmeg
8 spring onions, thinly sliced

2 × 15ml spoons/2 tablespoons chopped
parsley

TOPPING

50g/2 oz Gruyère **or** Edam cheese, grated
50g/2 oz medium oatmeal
2 × 15ml spoons/2 tablespoons jumbo
oats

Cook the swedes in boiling salted water for 20 minutes or until just tender. Drain and mash them, then beat in the porridge oats – they will absorb any excess moisture. Beat in the yoghurt, and season with salt, pepper and nutmeg. Stir in the spring onions and parsley, then transfer the mixture to a greased baking dish.

Mix together the ingredients for the topping, and sprinkle this over the swede mixture. Bake in a fairly hot oven, 190°C/375°F/Gas 5, for 35 minutes until the topping is crisp and brown. Serve hot.

PARSNIPS WITH TOASTED OATS

450g/1 lb parsnips, diced
salt, freshly ground pepper
4 × 15ml spoons/4 tablespoons low-fat
yoghurt
½ × 2.5ml spoon/¼ teaspoon grated
nutmeg

TOPPING

4 × 15ml spoons/4 tablespoons jumbo
oats
2 × 15ml spoons/2 tablespoons chopped
hazelnuts

GARNISH

sprigs parsley

Prepare the topping first. Mix the oats and hazelnuts, and grill under moderate heat for 4-5 minutes, stirring once or twice to brown the mixture evenly.

Cook the diced parsnips in boiling salted water for 20-25 minutes until very tender. Drain and mash them, then return the pan to moderate heat to evaporate the excess moisture. Beat in the yoghurt, then season with nutmeg, salt and pepper.

Spread the mashed parsnip mixture in a heated serving dish. Sprinkle the oats mixture on top, and garnish with the parsley. Serve at once.

VEGETABLE BURGERS

350g/12 oz potatoes, peeled
350g/12 oz parsnips
salt, freshly ground pepper
25g/1 oz sunflower margarine
1 medium onion, chopped
1 clove of garlic, crushed
1 × 5ml spoon/1 teaspoon curry powder
4 × 15ml spoons/4 tablespoons skimmed milk

1 × 15ml spoon/1 tablespoon chopped parsley
50g/2 oz chopped hazelnuts
50g/2 oz rolled porridge oats
2 × 15ml spoons/2 tablespoons sesame seeds
a pinch of grated nutmeg

Cook the potatoes and parsnips in boiling salted water until tender, then drain and mash them.

Meanwhile melt the margarine in a pan, and cook the onion and garlic over moderate heat for 3 minutes, stirring once or twice. Stir in the curry powder, and cook for 1 minute.

Beat the onion mixture into the mashed vegetables. Beat in the milk until it has been absorbed, then beat in the parsley and half the hazelnuts, oats and sesame seeds. Season the mixture with salt, pepper and nutmeg. Divide it into eight equal pieces, and shape them into rounds. Press flat to make burger shapes.

Mix together the remaining nuts, oats and sesame seeds. Turn the vegetable rounds in this mixture, pressing it well into the surface. Place them on a greased baking sheet, and cook in a fairly hot oven, 190°C/375°F/Gas 5, for 25 minutes or until well browned.

Variation
If preferred, the burgers can be dry-fried in a non-stick pan.

CAULIFLOWER CROWN

1 medium cauliflower
salt

DRESSING

2 × 15ml spoons/2 tablespoons sunflower oil
1 × 15ml spoon/1 tablespoon cider vinegar
1 × 2.5ml spoon/½ teaspoon lemon juice
1 × 2.5ml spoon/½ teaspoon dry English mustard
salt, freshly ground pepper

GARNISH

25g/1 oz sunflower margarine
4 × 15ml spoons/4 tablespoons jumbo oats
2 hard-boiled eggs
1 medium onion, chopped
2 × 15ml spoons/2 tablespoons chopped parsley

Cook the cauliflower in boiling salted water for 10-15 minutes until just tender, then drain well. Transfer to a heated serving dish, cover with foil and keep warm.

Meanwhile, mix together the ingredients for the dressing, and make the garnish. Melt the margarine in a pan, and fry the oats over moderate heat for 3-4 minutes, stirring constantly, until dry and toasted. Chop the egg whites, Sieve the yolks.

Pour the dressing over the cauliflower, then arrange rings of oats, egg white, egg yolk, chopped onion and parsley over the cauliflower. Serve at once.

VEGETABLE RAMEKINS

225g/8 oz cauliflower
225g/8 oz carrots
225g/8 oz peas
salt, freshly ground pepper
9 × 15ml spoons/9 tablespoons low-fat
yoghurt
a pinch of grated nutmeg
1 × 5ml spoon/1 teaspoon grated orange
rind

1 × 15ml spoon/1 tablespoon chopped
mint **or** 1 × 5ml spoon/1 teaspoon dried
mint

TOPPING

4 × 15ml spoons/4 tablespoons rolled
porridge oats
4 × 15ml spoons/4 tablespoons grated
Parmesan cheese

Cook the cauliflower, carrots and peas in separate pans of boiling salted water until tender. Drain the vegetables and mash each type separately. Season each purée with salt and pepper, then beat in 3 × 15ml spoons/3 tablespoons of the yoghurt. Add the grated nutmeg to the cauliflower purée. Beat the orange rind into the carrot purée. Beat the mint into the pea purée.

Make layers of the cauliflower, carrot and pea purées in four greased individual ramekin dishes.

Mix together the oats and cheese for the topping, and sprinkle over each dish. Cover with foil, and stand the dishes in a roasting pan half filled with boiling water. Cook them in a fairly hot oven, 190°C/375°F/Gas 5, for 20 minutes. Serve hot.

Note This dish makes an unusual and colourful first course, or a three-in-one vegetable accompaniment to roast or grilled meat and poultry.

HIGH-FIBRE ONIONS

4 large Spanish onions (175g/6 oz each
approx)
40g/1½ oz wholewheat breadcrumbs
40g/1½ oz pinhead oatmeal
1 × 15ml spoon/1 tablespoon chopped
parsley
1 × 5ml spoon/1 teaspoon dried oregano
50g/2 oz cashew nuts, chopped
50g/2 oz currants
3 × 15ml spoons/3 tablespoons orange
juice

2 × 5ml spoons/2 teaspoons grated
orange rind
salt, freshly ground pepper
4 × 15ml spoons/4 tablespoons
Greek-style yoghurt

TOPPING

2 × 15ml spoons/2 tablespoons jumbo
oats
4 × 15ml spoons/4 tablespoons grated
Parmesan cheese

Cook the onions in boiling water for 7 minutes, then drain and dry them. Open out the onions from the centre and, using a teaspoon, scoop out the centres, leaving firm 'walls'. Place the onions in a baking dish. Chop the onion centres.

Mix together the chopped onion, breadcrumbs, oatmeal, herbs, nuts, currants, orange juice and orange rind. Season the mixture with salt and pepper, then stir in the yoghurt. Pack the mixture into the onion centres.

Mix together the jumbo oats and cheese for the topping, and sprinkle on top of the filling. Cook in a fairly hot oven, 190°C/375°F/Gas 5, for 30 minutes until brown and bubbling. Serve at once, with roast or grilled poultry.

PEA-GREEN BOATS

225g/8 oz fresh peas
25g/1 oz sunflower margarine
4 × 15ml spoons/4 tablespoons chicken stock
1 small onion, finely chopped
salt, freshly ground pepper
40g/1½ oz fine oatmeal

1 × 15ml spoon/1 tablespoon low-fat yoghurt
2 × 15ml spoons/2 tablespoons chopped mint
675g/1½ lb canned artichoke bases, drained
sprigs mint

Put the peas in a pan with the margarine, stock and onion. Season with salt and pepper. Heat to boiling point, then cover the pan and simmer for 10 minutes or until the peas are tender and have absorbed most of the stock.

Liquidize the peas and any stock in a blender or press through a sieve. Blend in the oatmeal, yoghurt and mint, then season to taste.

Arrange the artichoke bases in a greased, shallow baking dish, and spoon or pipe in the pea purée. Heat the cases in a moderate oven, 180°C/350°F/Gas 5, for 10 minutes until bubbling. Garnish with the mint sprigs, and serve hot.

BRAISED VEGETABLES

2 × 15ml spoons/2 tablespoons olive oil
1 × 5ml spoon/1 teaspoon lemon juice
6 × 15ml spoons/6 tablespoons white wine
3 × 15ml spoons/3 tablespoons concentrated tomato purée
1 medium onion, thinly sliced
2 cloves garlic, finely chopped
1 × 5ml spoon/1 teaspoon coriander seeds
1 × 2.5ml spoon/½ teaspoon mustard seeds

2 dried red chillies
2 bay leaves
salt, freshly ground pepper
225g/8 oz button onions
4 stalks celery, cut into 3.75cm/1½ inch slices
175g/6 oz button mushrooms, sliced
½ small cauliflower, cut into florets
4 × 15ml spoons/4 tablespoons jumbo oats
2 × 15ml spoons/2 tablespoons chopped parsley

Put the oil, lemon juice, wine, tomato purée, onion, garlic, seeds, chillies, bay leaves and seasoning into a pan, stir well and heat to boiling point. Cover the pan and simmer for 20 minutes. Add the button onions, celery, mushrooms and cauliflower florets, and return to boiling point. Cover and cook for 15 minutes, then stir in the jumbo oats. Season to taste, then cook for a further 5 minutes. Discard the bay leaves. Stir in the parsley. Serve warm, as an accompaniment to roast or grilled meats.

Variation
The recipe can be chilled and served, Greek style, as a starter.

FENNEL IN CHEESE SAUCE

3 medium bulbs fennel, sliced
salt, freshly ground pepper

SAUCE

25g/1 oz sunflower margarine
25g/1 oz fine oatmeal
200ml/7 fl oz buttermilk
100g/4 oz low-fat curd cheese
2 × 15ml spoons/2 tablespoons chopped
parsley
a pinch of grated nutmeg

TOPPING

50g/2 oz jumbo oats
50g/2 oz Gruyère **or** Edam cheese, grated

GARNISH (optional)

sprays of fennel

Cook the fennel in boiling salted water for about 5 minutes or until just tender. Drain thoroughly (reserving the stock for a sauce or soup), and pat dry. Arrange in a greased, shallow baking dish.

To make the sauce, melt the margarine in a pan, and stir in the oatmeal until it forms a smooth paste. Stir in the buttermilk, stirring constantly, and heat to boiling point, then simmer for 3 minutes. Beat in the cheese and parsley, a little at a time, then season with salt, pepper and nutmeg. Pour the sauce over the fennel.

Mix together the oats and cheese for the topping, and sprinkle this over the sauce. Cook in a moderate oven, 180°C/350°F/Gas 4, for 20 minutes until brown and bubbling. Garnish, if liked, with the fennel leaves. Serve hot.

CRISPY BRUSSELS SPROUTS

450g/1 lb Brussels sprouts
salt, freshly ground pepper
2 × 15ml spoons/2 tablespoons orange
juice
1 × 5ml spoon/1 teaspoon grated orange
rind
2 × 15ml spoons/2 tablespoons low-fat
yoghurt

TOPPING

15g/½ oz sunflower margarine
2 × 15ml spoons/2 tablespoons
sunflower oil
1 small onion, finely chopped
25g/1 oz jumbo oats
25g/1 oz chopped walnuts

Steam the Brussels sprouts over boiling salted water for 12-15 minutes or until barely tender.

Mix together the orange juice, orange rind and yoghurt, and season with salt and pepper. Simmer the vegetables in the sauce for 2-3 minutes until the liquid has almost evaporated.

To make the topping, heat the margarine and oil in a pan, and cook the onion over moderate heat for 2 minutes, stirring frequently. Add the oats and walnuts, and cook over moderate heat for 2-3 minutes, stirring all the time. Sprinkle the topping over the vegetables, and serve at once.

BAKED AVOCADO PEARS

2 medium avocado pears, halved and stoned
2 × 5ml spoons/2 teaspoons lemon juice
125g/5 oz low-fat soft cheese
2 medium cooked carrots, diced
2 × 15ml spoons/2 tablespoons jumbo oats
50g/2 oz chopped walnuts

1 × 5ml spoon/1 teaspoon snipped chives
salt, freshly ground pepper

GARNISH

sprigs parsley
walnut halves

Brush the cut surfaces of the avocado pears with the lemon juice. Beat the cheese until soft, then stir in the carrots, oats, walnuts and chives. Season with salt and pepper. Divide the filling between the avocado halves. Wrap each one in foil, and place in a shallow baking dish. Cook in a fairly hot oven, 190°C/375°F/Gas 5, for 20 minutes until bubbling. Serve at once, garnished with the parsley sprigs and walnuts.

Note This unusual, hot avocado dish is good with baked or grilled fish, or with white meat such as chicken and veal. It also makes an attractive starter.

OAT BIRIANI

SERVES 4-6

225g/8 oz oat groats, soaked and drained
2 × 15ml spoons/2 tablespoons sunflower oil
2 medium onions, thinly sliced
2 cloves garlic, crushed
2 stalks celery, thinly sliced
1 × 2.5ml spoon/½ teaspoon ground turmeric
1 × 2.5ml spoon/½ teaspoon ground ginger
1 × 2.5ml spoon/½ teaspoon ground cumin
½ × 2.5ml spoon/¼ teaspoon Cayenne pepper
salt

1 × 15ml spoon/1 tablespoon concentrated tomato purée
150ml/¼ pint hot chicken stock
2 medium carrots, diced
½ small cauliflower, cut into florets
100g/4 oz button mushrooms, thinly sliced
2 large tomatoes, skinned and chopped
75g/3 oz seedless raisins
50g/2 oz blanched almonds

GARNISH

lemon wedges

Cook the groats in boiling unsalted water for 1 hour, then drain them.

Heat the oil in a pan, and fry the onions, garlic and celery over moderate heat for 2 minutes. Stir in the spices and salt, and cook for 1 minute, then add the tomato purée and stock, stirring constantly. Add the drained groats, the carrots and cauliflower, heat to boiling point, then cover and simmer for 10 minutes. Add the mushrooms and tomatoes, and cook for a further 3-4 minutes. Stir in the raisins, and heat through. Scatter the almonds on top. Serve hot, garnished with the lemon wedges.

Note This is a good accompaniment to spiced meat dishes or to vegetable kebabs.

CURRIED OAT RING

175g/6 oz oat groats, soaked and drained
175g/6 oz canned pimentos, drained and
sliced
1 green pepper, de-seeded and chopped
3 tomatoes, skinned, de-seeded and
chopped
3 spring onions, chopped
4 × 15ml spoons/4 tablespoons sultanas
8 dried apricots, chopped
2 × 15ml spoons/2 tablespoons seedless
raisins
2 × 15ml spoons/2 tablespoons blanched
chopped almonds
oil for brushing

DRESSING

2 × 15ml spoons/2 tablespoons
sunflower oil
2 × 15ml spoons/2 tablespoons red wine
vinegar
1 × 15ml spoon/1 tablespoon lemon
juice
1 × 5ml spoon/1 teaspoon curry powder
1 clove of garlic, crushed
2 × 15ml spoons/2 tablespoons low-fat
yoghurt
salt, freshly ground pepper

Cook the groats in boiling water for 1¼-1½ hours, then drain thoroughly and rinse under cold running water. Drain again, then leave to cool.

Cut one pimento slice into 1.25cm/½ inch diamond shapes, and put to one side. Chop the remainder, then mix together with the groats, pepper, tomatoes, spring onions, dried fruit and almonds.

Mix together the ingredients for the dressing until well blended, and pour this over the groats mixture.

Brush a 600ml/1 pint ring mould with oil. Arrange the reserved pimento diamond shapes in the base. Pack the oat salad into the mould, then cover and chill for at least 1½ hours.

Run a knife blade around the inside of the mould, and turn out on to a serving plate.

Serve with other salads or to accompany cold or grilled meats.

OPPOSITE *Green Salad with Oat Dressing, Bean Salad (page 78) and Curried Oat Ring*

GREEN SALAD WITH OAT DRESSING

SERVES 6

1 small curly endive
1 head of chicory
1 bulb of fennel, thinly sliced
4 spring onions, thinly sliced
½ small cucumber, thinly sliced

DRESSING

3 × 15ml spoons/3 tablespoons olive oil
3 × 15ml spoons/3 tablespoons cider vinegar
2 × 15ml spoons/ 2 tablespoons low-fat yoghurt
½ × 2.5ml spoon/¼ teaspoon dry English mustard
salt, freshly ground pepper
3 × 15ml spoons/3 tablespoons jumbo oats

Prepare the dressing first. Mix together the oil, vinegar, yoghurt and mustard until well blended. Season with salt and pepper, then stir in the oats. Put to one side for at least 1 hour.

Meanwhile, discard the outer leaves of the endive and chicory. Tear off each leaf, and tear in half any very large ones. Toss together the endive, chicory, fennel, onions and cucumber. If the salad is to be stored before serving, put it in a polythene bag in a refrigerator.

Just before serving, pour the dressing over the salad, and toss to coat the leaves thoroughly. Serve in a chilled bowl.

AUBERGINE SALAD WITH OAT DRESSING

SERVES 4-6

1 large aubergine
1 medium courgette, thinly sliced
100g/4 oz button mushrooms, thinly sliced

DRESSING

5 × 15ml spoons/5 tablespoons low-fat yoghurt
3 × 15ml spoons/3 tablespoons orange juice
2 × 15ml spoons/2 tablespoons sunflower seeds

2 × 15ml spoons/2 tablespoons pinhead oatmeal
2 × 15ml spoons/2 tablespoons chopped parsley
1 clove of garlic, crushed
salt, freshly ground pepper

GARNISH

orange wedges

Prepare the dressing first. Beat the yoghurt until smooth, then beat in the orange juice. Stir in the sunflower seeds, oatmeal, parsley and garlic, and season with salt and pepper. Put to one side for at least 1 hour.

Meanwhile, prick the aubergine all over with a fork, then grill under high heat for about 20 minutes, turning frequently so that it is almost black on all sides. Hold it under cold running water, then peel off the skin and thinly slice it. Leave to cool.

Toss together the aubergine, courgette and mushroom slices, then pour on the dressing, and toss to coat the vegetables thoroughly. Garnish with the orange wedges.

Note This salad makes a good accompaniment to grilled lamb dishes, such as kebabs.

OAT SALAD WITH COURGETTES

6 courgettes, thinly sliced
salt
125g/5 oz cooked oat groats
4 medium tomatoes, skinned and chopped
2 × 15ml spoons/2 tablespoons pumpkin seeds
6 stuffed olives, chopped
lemon wedges

DRESSING

3 × 15ml spoons/3 tablespoons olive oil
2 × 15ml spoons/2 tablespoons red wine vinegar
1 × 15ml spoon/1 tablespoon chopped mint
1 × 5ml spoon/1 teaspoon chopped basil
or 1 × 2.5ml spoon/½ teaspoon dried basil
salt, freshly ground pepper

Blanch the courgette slices in salted water for 2 minutes, then drain them and pat dry. Leave to cool.

Meanwhile, mix together the ingredients for the dressing until well blended.

Toss together the cooled courgette slices, the groats, tomatoes, pumpkin seeds and olives. Pour on the dressing, and toss well. Garnish with the lemon wedges.

Note Serve this vegetable and oat dish as part of a salad meal or to accompany grilled fish or meats.

GREEN OAT SALAD

SERVES 4-6

175g/6 oz oat groats, soaked and drained
175g/6 oz parsley, chopped
spinach **or** lettuce leaves
4 large tomatoes, sliced

DRESSING

3 × 15ml spoons/3 tablespoons olive oil
4 × 15ml spoons/4 tablespoons lemon
juice

1 × 5ml spoon/1 teaspoon grated lemon
rind
2 cloves garlic, crushed
6 spring onions, thinly sliced
salt, freshly ground pepper

GARNISH

lemon slices

Cook the oat groats in boiling water for 1¼-1½ hours, then drain thoroughly and rinse under cold running water. Drain again, then toss the oats on a tea-towel to dry them well. Leave to cool.

Meanwhile, prepare the dressing. Mix together the oil, lemon juice, lemon rind and garlic. Stir in the onions, and season with salt and pepper.

Stir together the groats and parsley, pour on the dressing, and mix well.

Line a serving dish with spinach or lettuce leaves. Pile the salad in the centre, and arrange the tomato slices around the outside. Garnish with the lemon slices.

Note Serve as part of a cold meal or as a vegetarian starter.

SPROUTED OATS

You can make crisp, crunchy salad shoots, like bean shoots, by germinating oat grains. The sprouts are not only rich in proteins and vitamins — especially Vitamin C which is not present in the ungerminated grain — they are also delicious!

3 × 15ml spoons/3 tablespoons oat groats
warm water

Soak the oat groats overnight in a bowl of warm water, then drain. Place the seeds in a 900g/2 lb preserving jar, and fill with warm water. Cover the jar with a piece of muslin, cheesecloth or similar material, and secure it with a rubber band or string. Shake the jar and drain off the water. Put the jar on its side in a dark place, such as a drawer.

Fill the jar with warm water each day, shake well, drain off the water, and return to a dark place. The groats should sprout in about 5 days.

Use the sprouted oats when the shoots are about 2.5cm/1 inch long.

Serve raw with other salad ingredients, stir-fry with vegetables or steam over boiling stock.

Note Sprouted oats *must* be served crisp.

STIR-FRIED OATS

225g/8 oz mange-tout peas
salt
2 × 15ml spoons/2 tablespoons peanut oil
2 thin slices fresh root ginger, finely chopped
4 spring onions, thinly sliced
2 cloves garlic, finely chopped
4 stalks tender celery, thinly sliced
100g/4 oz sprouted oats (page 77)
100g/4 oz cashew nuts

SAUCE

1 × 15ml spoon/1 tablespoon soy sauce
2 × 15ml spoons/2 tablespoons medium sherry
2 × 15ml spoons/2 tablespoons chicken stock
freshly ground pepper
a pinch of ground ginger

Blanch the mange-tout peas in boiling salted water for 2 minutes, then drain and pat dry. Mix together the ingredients for the sauce.

Heat the oil in a heavy-based pan or wok, and stir-fry the ginger, onions, garlic and celery over high heat for 30 seconds. Add the mange-tout and sprouted oats, and stir-fry for 1 minute. Pour on the sauce, heat to boiling point, stirring constantly, then simmer for 2 minutes. Stir in the cashew nuts. Serve at once.

BEAN SALAD

SERVES 6

100g/4 oz dried red kidney beans, soaked and drained (see **Note**)
100g/4 oz dried black **or** flageolet beans, soaked and drained (see **Note**)
225g/8 oz sprouted oats (page 77)
2 stalks celery, thinly sliced
onion rings
sprigs parsley

DRESSING

3 × 15ml spoons/3 tablespoons sunflower oil
3 × 15ml spoons/3 tablespoons orange juice
1 × 5ml spoon/1 teaspoon lemon juice
½ × 2.5ml spoon/¼ teaspoon dry English mustard
1 clove of garlic, crushed
salt, freshly ground pepper

Boil the kidney beans and the black beans briskly in separate pans of fresh water for 10 minutes, then cook for 1 hour or until tender.

Meanwhile, mix together the ingredients for the dressing until well blended.

Drain the cooked beans, mix them together, and toss at once in the dressing. Leave to cool.

Stir the sprouted oats and celery into the cooled beans, then transfer the salad to a serving dish. Scatter with the onion rings, and garnish with the parsley sprigs.

Note It is important to discard the draining water used for soaking the dried beans.

A 'Sweet' Tooth

There's no doubt about it that it's the dessert course that presents the most difficulty in a healthy eating plan: if you choose to have a prepared dessert at all, that is. It has to be said that you can't beat a selection of fresh fruits – those delicious, colourful, tempting all-shapes-and-sizes packages of nutrition, fibre and flavour. But there are times when family and friends, the cook too, like to round off a meal with 'something for a change'.

This chapter looks on the bright side, at the various types of desserts that will satisfy the 'sweet tooths' among us, without devastating the calorie bank.

Dried fruits of all kinds are an absolute boon, packed as they are with natural fruit sugars; fibre, too. Most dried fruits have approximately ten times the fibre content, weight for weight, of their fresh counterparts.

Borrow this extra-sweetness of dried apricots, peaches, pears and dates by mixing them with tangy fresh fruits. Make a light purée of dried fruits, and poach sliced apples or pears in it; no need for sugar then. And you can even dry dates until they are drier still, and grind them to a coarse powder which is a very acceptable sugar substitute (see recipe on page 89).

And where do oats come in? Tossed with soft fruits into whipped yoghurt to simulate a Scottish favourite; layered in a summer pudding to soak up the full flavour of the soft fruit juices; stirred into simmered soft fruit to thicken it until it 'sways'; as crunchy and cobbler toppings; fillings for apples and peaches; and even blended with yoghurt in a dairy dressing to serve with grilled fruit kebabs.

LOWLAND CROWDIE

4 × 15ml spoons/4 tablespoons medium oatmeal
4 × 15ml spoons/4 tablespoons jumbo **or** rolled porridge oats
300ml/½ pint low-fat yoghurt
1 × 15ml spoon/1 tablespoon clear honey, melted
225g/8 oz raspberries, hulled

Toast the oatmeal and the oats separately under moderate heat for about 4 minutes, stirring frequently, until evenly brown. Leave to cool.

Beat the yoghurt until smooth, and stir in the honey, most of the raspberries and the cooled oatmeal. Divide the mixture between four individual serving dishes, sprinkle the toasted oats on top, and decorate with the reserved raspberries.

OAT FRUMENTY

SERVES 6

175g/6 oz oat groats, soaked and drained
600ml/1 pint skimmed milk
2 eggs
1 × 15ml spoon/1 tablespoon clear honey

100g/4 oz seedless raisins
2 × 5ml spoons/2 teaspoons lemon rind
½ × 2.5ml spoon/¼ teaspoon ground mace
a pinch of grated nutmeg

Cook the groats in boiling water for 1¼ hours, then drain thoroughly, rinse under cold running water, and drain again. Put the groats into a greased 900ml/1½ pint pie dish.

Beat together the milk, eggs and honey, and pour this over the groats. Stir in the raisins, lemon rind, mace and nutmeg. Bake in a warm oven, 160°C/320°F/Gas 3, for 1 hour until set. Serve hot or cold.

Note A drizzle of honey on top is traditional with this simple pudding which dates back to Roman times.

BLACKCURRANT KISSEL

675g/1½ lb blackcurrants, stripped from stalks
2 × 15ml spoons/2 tablespoons water
a pinch of ground cinnamon
2 × 15ml spoons/2 tablespoons date 'sugar' (page 89) **or** clear honey
2 × 15ml spoons/2 tablespoons fine oatmeal

DECORATION

scented geranium **or** herb leaves

Put the blackcurrants, water, cinnamon and date 'sugar' or honey in a pan. Heat slowly to boiling point, stirring occasionally to dissolve the honey.

Stir a little of the juice from the pan into the oatmeal to make a thick paste. Add more, stirring constantly, until the mixture is the consistency of single cream, then pour it into the fruit. Stir over moderate heat until the mixture thickens. Pour the fruit into a heatproof serving dish, and leave to cool. Decorate the dish with the leaves, and serve with low-fat yoghurt or cottage cheese.

Variations
Other fruits are equally good cooked and served in this way. Try rhubarb, redcurrants, raspberries or blackberries.

FRUIT KEBABS

12 dried apricots, soaked and drained
8 no-pre-soak prunes, stoned
1 orange, divided into segments, pith and skin removed
2 dessert apples, cored and quartered

MARINADE

4 × 15ml spoons/4 tablespoons orange juice
1 × 5ml spoon/1 teaspoon grated orange rind
1 × 15ml spoon/1 tablespoon chopped mint

1 × 15ml spoon/1 tablespoon sunflower oil

DRESSING

100g/4 oz cottage cheese
3 × 15ml spoons/3 tablespoons rolled porridge oats
4 × 15ml spoons/4 tablespoons orange juice
1 × 5ml spoon/1 teaspoon grated orange rind
5 × 15ml spoons/5 tablespoons low-fat yoghurt

Divide the fruit between four skewers, alternating between fresh and dried fruits and differing colours. Place the skewers in a shallow ovenproof dish.

Mix together the marinade ingredients. Pour this over the skewers, turn them to coat the fruit thoroughly, then put to one side for at least 1 hour.

Meanwhile, liquidize the dressing ingredients in a blender. Alternatively, sieve the cheese and beat in the remaining ingredients. Chill the dressing.

Grill the skewers under moderate heat for 5-6 minutes until the fruit is well browned. Serve at once, accompanied by the dressing.

GOLDEN FRUIT SALAD

1 × 5ml spoon/1 teaspoon coriander seeds
5cm/2 inch piece of cinnamon stick
1 × 15ml spoon/1 tablespoon clear honey
600ml/1 pint water

150ml/¼ pint white wine
350g/12 oz mixed dried fruits, eg apple rings, apricots, peaches, pears, prunes
50g/2 oz seedless raisins
50g/2 oz jumbo oats, toasted

Put the coriander seeds, cinnamon, honey and water into a pan, and heat slowly to boiling point. Boil for 10 minutes, then add the wine and mixed dried fruit, and simmer for 1 hour until the fruit is tender. Stir in the raisins, and cook for a further 5 minutes, then discard the cinnamon stick. Just before serving, scatter on the toasted oats. Serve hot or cold, with low-fat yoghurt.

APRICOT FOLLY

175g/6 oz dried apricot pieces, soaked and drained
125g/5 oz cottage cheese
150ml/¼ pint low-fat yoghurt
75g/3 oz rolled porridge oats **or** jumbo oats
2 × 15ml spoons/2 tablespoons Amaretti liqueur (optional)

DECORATION

4 fresh apricots
8 small bay leaves

Liquidize the apricots with the cheese, yoghurt, oats and liqueur, if used. Divide the purée between four individual glasses, and decorate each one with a fresh apricot and the bay leaves. Serve chilled, with Oat Cakes (see page 20).

Variations
You can use other well-flavoured fruit purées for this smooth, satisfying dessert. Blackcurrant purée, flavoured with a little cassis, is excellent.

PRAIRIE ICEBOX DESSERT

SERVES 4-6

2 egg yolks
300ml/½ pint low-fat yoghurt
300ml/½ pint apricot purée (see **Note**)
50g/2 oz rolled porridge oats, toasted
blanched almonds, toasted and chopped

Beat the egg yolks with the yoghurt until the mixture is creamy. Gradually beat in the apricot purée, then stir in the toasted oats. Turn the mixture into a chilled container such as a 450g/1 lb loaf tin. Cover with foil, and freeze for 1 hour.

Turn the partly frozen mixture into a chilled bowl, and beat well to break down the ice crystals. Return it to the container, cover and freeze for a further 3 hours.

To turn out the dessert, rinse out a tea-towel in warm water, wring well, and wrap round the container. Turn out the frozen dessert on to a serving dish, and press on the toasted almonds. Leave to rest in the refrigerator for 30 minutes before serving, cut in slices.

This dessert is particularly good accompanied by soft fruit such as strawberries and raspberries.

Note Apricot purée is available in tins as baby food. Alternatively, it can be made by soaking 125g/5 oz dried apricot pieces in 150ml/¼ pint water for 2 hours, then liquidizing both fruit and liquid in a blender or pressing it through a sieve.

OPPOSITE *Apricot Folly, Lowland Crowdie (page 79) and Prairie Icebox Dessert*

APPLE AND GINGER CRUNCH

450g/1 lb cooking apples, peeled, cored
and thinly sliced
100g/4 oz dried apricot pieces, soaked,
drained and chopped
4 × 15ml spoons/4 tablespoons orange
juice
1 × 5ml spoon/1 teaspoon grated orange
rind

TOPPING

75g/3 oz wholewheat flour
25g/1 oz medium oatmeal
1 × 5ml spoon/1 teaspoon ground ginger
50g/2 oz sunflower margarine
25g/1 oz Demerara sugar
50g/2 oz rolled porridge oats
1 × 2.5ml spoon/½ teaspoon coriander
seeds, lightly crushed

Put the apples, apricots, orange juice and rind into a 900ml/1½ pint pie dish.
To prepare the topping, mix together the flour, oatmeal and ginger, then rub in the margarine. Stir in the sugar, rolled oats and coriander seeds. Sprinkle the mixture over the fruit, and bake in a fairly hot oven, 190°C/375°F/Gas 5, for 35 minutes until the topping is crisp and golden. Serve hot, warm or cold – it's equally delicious.

CIDER-BAKED APPLES

4 large cooking apples
6 × 15ml spoons/6 tablespoons medium cider

FILLING

75g/3 oz stoned dried dates, finely chopped
2 × 15ml spoons/2 tablespoons jumbo oats
1 × 15ml spoon/1 tablespoon lemon juice
1 × 5ml spoon/1 teaspoon grated lemon rind

Core the apples, taking care to remove all the tough, inedible parts. Run a sharp knife round the centre circumference of the skin to prevent the fruit from bursting. Place the apples in a baking dish that just fits them.
Mix together the dates, oats, lemon juice and lemon rind until the filling is well blended. Pack the filling into the apples, and pile it into a dome on top.
Pour the cider over the apples, and cook them in a moderate oven, 180°C/350°F/Gas 4, basting them occasionally, for 45 minutes or until the apples are just beginning to soften. Do not let them collapse. Serve hot, with low-fat yoghurt.

CARROT PUDDING

50g/2 oz wholewheat breadcrumbs
50g/2 oz fine oatmeal
25g/1 oz rolled porridge oats
100g/4 oz carrots, grated
50g/2 oz ground almonds
a pinch of grated nutmeg
1 × 2.5ml spoon/½ teaspoon ground cinnamon

3 × 15ml spoons/3 tablespoons orange juice
2 × 5ml spoons/2 teaspoons grated orange rind
50g/2 oz seedless raisins
50g/2 oz sultanas
50g/2 oz walnuts, chopped
2 eggs, separated

Mix together the breadcrumbs, oatmeal, oats, grated carrot, almonds and spices. Stir in the orange juice and rind, the raisins, sultanas and walnuts. Beat the egg yolks, then beat them into the mixture. Whisk the egg whites until stiff, then fold them into the mixture.

Turn the mixture into a greased 900ml/1½ pint pudding basin. Cover the top with foil and tie securely. Stand the basin on a trivet in a large pan with boiling water which comes half-way up the sides. Cover the pan, and boil for 1¾ hours, topping up with more boiling water as required.

Run a knife around the pudding, then turn it out carefully on to a heated serving dish. Serve hot, with low-fat yoghurt or soured cream.

SUMMER PUDDING

100g/4 oz dried pears, soaked
225g/8 oz raspberries, hulled
225g/8 oz blackcurrants, stripped from stalks
1 × 15ml spoon/1 tablespoon date 'sugar' (page 89) **or** clear honey
6-7 slices wholewheat bread, crusts removed
8 × 15ml spoons/8 tablespoons rolled porridge oats

Cook the pears in their soaking water for 30 minutes. Drain them, and reserve 3 × 15ml spoons/3 tablespoons of the liquid. Chop the pears.

Put the raspberries, blackcurrants and date 'sugar' or honey in a pan. Heat to boiling point in the reserved liquid, then simmer for 5 minutes. Stir in the chopped pears.

Line a greased 600ml/1 pint bowl with some of the bread slices, cutting them so that there are no gaps.

Set aside 4 × 15ml spoons/4 tablespoons of the juice remaining from cooking the fruit. Fill the lined bowl with the fruit and its juice, sprinkling the oats between each 'layer'. Cover the top of the bowl completely with the remaining bread slices cut to fit. Place a saucer to fit inside the rim of the bowl, and stand a heavy weight on it – eg a filled food can. Chill overnight in a refrigerator.

Run a knife around the pudding, and turn it out on to a plate. Spoon over the reserved fruit juice to cover any unsoaked areas of bread. Cut the pudding into wedges, and serve with low-fat yoghurt or soured cream.

NORTH SEA PANCAKES

MAKES 4

100g/4 oz wholewheat flour
salt
300ml/½ pint orange juice
2 eggs
1 × 5ml spoon/1 teaspoon grated orange
rind
4 × 15ml spoons/4 tablespoons rolled
porridge oats
175g/6 oz dried apricot pieces
oil for frying

FILLING

225g/8 oz low-fat cottage cheese
1 × 15ml spoon/1 tablespoon orange
juice
1 × 5ml spoon/1 teaspoon grated orange
rind

DECORATION (optional)

orange wedges

Mix together the flour and salt. Gradually beat in the orange juice and then the eggs, one at a time. Stir in the orange rind, oats and apricot pieces.

Beat the cottage cheese for the filling until smooth, then beat in the orange juice and rind.

Lightly brush a non-stick omelet pan with oil, if necessary. Heat the pan over moderate heat, and pour in just enough of the batter to cover the base. Shake the pan, and cook the batter for 2-3 minutes until it bubbles and the underside is brown. Flip or toss the pancake, and cook until the other side is brown. Keep the cooked pancake warm while cooking the remaining batter.

Spread the filling over half of each pancake. Fold them over in half, and then in half again. Serve at once, accompanied, if liked, by the orange wedges.

BAKED PEACHES

SERVES 6

6 large, ripe peaches, skinned, halved and
stoned

FILLING

50g/2 oz ground almonds
25g/1 oz rolled porridge oats **or** jumbo
oats
1 × 2.5ml spoon/½ teaspoon ground
cinnamon

1 × 5ml spoon/1 teaspoon grated orange
rind
50g/2 oz sunflower margarine

SAUCE

225g/8 oz raspberries, hulled
2 × 15ml spoons/2 tablespoons clear
honey

Prepare the filling first. Mix together the almonds, oats, cinnamon and orange rind, then rub in the margarine. Spread the filling over the cut sides of the peaches, packing it firmly into the cavities.

To make the sauce, heat the raspberries and honey until they just reach boiling point, then pour the sauce into a baking dish.

Arrange the peaches, filled sides up, in the dish, and bake in a fairly hot oven, 190°C/375°F/Gas 5, for about 20 minutes until the filling is brown and bubbling. Serve hot.

OPPOSITE *North Sea Pancakes*

BANANA AND APPLE TART

SERVES 6

225g/8 oz cottage cheese
50g/2 oz rolled porridge oats
1 × 5ml spoon/1 teaspoon grated lemon rind
1 × 2.5ml spoon/½ teaspoon ground cinnamon
2 bananas, mashed
50g/2 oz dried mulberries **or** sultanas
2 dessert apples, cored and thinly sliced
2 × 15ml spoons/2 tablespoons clear honey, melted

OATMEAL PASTRY

175g/6 oz wholewheat flour
50g/2 oz fine oatmeal **plus** extra for rolling
2 × 5ml spoons/2 teaspoons baking powder
salt
1 × 5ml spoon/1 teaspoon ground cinnamon
100g/4 oz sunflower margarine
3 × 15ml spoons/3 tablespoons low-fat yoghurt

Make the pastry first. Mix together the flour, oatmeal, baking powder, salt and cinnamon, then rub in the margarine. Stir in the yoghurt, and form the mixture into a dough. Lightly dust a sheet of greaseproof paper with fine oatmeal. Roll out the dough to 6mm/¼ inch thickness, and use to line a 20cm/8 inch square baking tin. Trim the edges, and prick the base with a fork.

Mix together the cheese, oats, lemon rind and cinnamon. Spread the mixture over the pastry case. Mix the bananas and mulberries or sultanas, and spread the fruit over the cheese. Arrange the apple slices in rows on top, and brush them with the melted honey. Bake in a fairly hot oven, 190°C/375°F/Gas 5, for 40 minutes until lightly browned. Serve cold.

Note Low-fat yoghurt beaten with a mashed banana and a few drops of lemon juice makes a good accompaniment.

ATHOLL BROSE

Named after the 15th century Duke of Atholl, this dessert was originally made of thickly whipped cream spooned over the potent drink by which means he is said to have defeated his enemy.

750ml/1¼ pints Greek-style yoghurt, chilled
4 × 15ml spoons/4 tablespoons jumbo oats, toasted

LIQUID BASE

25g/1 oz pinhead **or** medium oatmeal
200ml/7 fl oz water
2 × 15ml spoons/2 tablespoons clear honey
300ml/½ pint whisky

First make the liquid base. Soak the oatmeal in the water for about 1 hour, then press it through a fine sieve, and discard the oatmeal. Gradually pour the liquid on to the honey, stirring constantly. Pour the mixture into a bottle, pour on the whisky, and shake well. Cover the bottle and store in a cool place. Shake it occasionally and always before using.

Pour 2 × 15ml spoons/2 tablespoons of the whisky mixture into each of four individual serving glasses. Spoon on the yoghurt. Scatter the toasted oats on top.

Note The liquid base can be stored in a screw-topped bottle to use over several months.

RHUBARB AND PEAR COBBLER

SERVES 6

225g/8 oz dried pears, soaked
450g/1 lb rhubarb, cut into 5cm/2 inch
slices
1 × 15ml spoon/1 tablespoon date
'sugar' (optional)
3 × 15ml spoons/3 tablespoons medium
oatmeal

TOPPING

175g/6 oz wholewheat flour
50g/2 oz fine oatmeal **plus** extra for
rolling

salt
1 × 2.5ml spoon/½ teaspoon ground
cinnamon
50g/2 oz sunflower margarine
75g/3 oz dried mulberries **or** sultanas
25g/1 oz Demerara sugar (optional)
150ml/¼ pint (approx) low-fat yoghurt
milk for brushing
2 × 15ml spoons/2 tablespoons medium
oatmeal

Cook the pears in their soaking water for 30 minutes. Drain them, reserving the liquid. Put the pears, rhubarb, 4 × 15ml spoons/4 tablespoons of the reserved juice and the date 'sugar' if used, into a 900ml/1½ pint pie dish. Stir in the oatmeal.

To make the topping, mix together the flour, fine oatmeal, salt and cinnamon. Rub in the margarine, then stir in the dried fruit and sugar, if used. Pour on just enough of the yoghurt to make a firm dough.

Roll out the dough on a surface lightly sprinkled with fine oatmeal, to a thickness of 1.25cm/½ inch, and cut out the dough into circles with a 6.25cm/2½ inch round cutter. Re-roll the trimmings and cut out more circles. Arrange the scone circles, slightly overlapping, over the fruit. Brush with milk, then sprinkle with the medium oatmeal. Bake in a fairly hot oven, 200°C/400°F/Gas 6, for 30-35 minutes until the scone topping is well risen and golden-brown. Serve hot, with low-fat yoghurt or soured cream.

DATE 'SUGAR'

MAKES 225g/8 oz (approx)

You can make a high-fibre powder with the sweetness of natural sugar by drying and grinding dates.

450g/1 lb whole dried dates, stoned

Spread the dates in a single layer, and each one separate, on a baking tray. Bake them in a very cool oven, 120°C/250°F/Gas ½, for about 12 hours, turning them occasionally, until they are very hard and light in weight. They should lose about half their weight.

Grind a few dates at a time by dropping them on to the revolving blades of a blender or food processor. Store the coarse powder in an airtight tin.

Note When making baked dishes, soak the date 'sugar' in the liquid ingredients for 10 minutes to prevent it from burning.

The Waft of Baking

Oat cakes, griddle scones, flip-and-toss pancakes, thin, flat breads like pitta, and moist breads spiced with ginger have been firmly established in the oat cuisine of northern Europe where oats have flourished for so many centuries. Yet flat heavy breads were the order of the day until improved strains of wheat with rising properties were available which would withstand low temperatures and heavy rains.

Despite their many virtues, the poor rising properties of oats produce a bread with a pleasant, slightly yoghurty flavour, but no bounce. Yet mixed with wholewheat flour and supplemented, if you like, with an extra raising agent, you have the best of both worlds: a loaf with the raising properties of wheat, the added flavour of oats, and both the insoluble and soluble fibre provided by the two grains.

If you are trying to restrict your fat and sugar intake, alas the Scottish flapjacks, Danish lace biscuits and lakeland gingerbreads are not for you. Try instead the soda bread flavoured with cheese and herbs; the scones sweetened with fresh and dried fruits and sometimes a spoonful of date 'sugar' (see page 89); the moist tea breads, which are heavenly sliced and spread with cottage cheese; the light-as-air muffins, and the plain, ordinary and very delicious oat bread – the perfect accompaniment to soups and salads.

APRICOT SCONE ROUND

MAKES 6 SLICES

25g/1 oz date 'sugar' (page 89)
150ml/¼ pint buttermilk
175g/6 oz wholewheat self-raising flour
50g/2 oz fine oatmeal **plus** extra for dusting
2 × 15ml spoons/2 tablespoons rolled porridge oats
1 × 5ml spoon/1 teaspoon baking powder

salt
½ × 2.5ml spoon/¼ teaspoon ground allspice
40g/1½ oz sunflower margarine
100g/4 oz dried apricot pieces
milk for brushing

Soak the date 'sugar' in the buttermilk for at least 10 minutes.

Mix together the dry ingredients. Rub in the margarine, then stir in the apricot pieces. Pour on just enough of the sweetened buttermilk to make a firm dough.

Shape the dough into a round on a surface lightly sprinkled with oatmeal, then press it into a 17.5cm/7 inch round tin. Mark into six wedges, and brush the top with milk. Bake in a hot oven, 220°C/425°F/Gas 7, for 20-25 minutes until well risen and golden-brown. Cool slightly in the tin, then turn out on to a wire rack. Serve warm, if possible.

Note Cottage cheese is a good 'spread'.

Apple Scones (page 95), Banana Tea Bread, Cheese and Herb Soda Bread (page 93) and Oat Plait (page 92)

BANANA TEA BREAD

MAKES ONE 17.5cm/7 inch SQUARE LOAF

100g/4 oz date 'sugar' (page 89)
3 eggs
75g/3 oz sunflower margarine
3 large bananas, mashed
½ × 2.5ml spoon/¼ teaspoon vanilla
essence
300g/10 oz wholewheat flour

100g/4 oz fine oatmeal
2 × 5ml spoons/2 teaspoons baking
powder
salt
100g/4 oz ground hazelnuts
2 × 15ml spoons/2 tablespoons pinhead
oatmeal

Beat the date 'sugar' into the eggs, and put to one side for at least 10 minutes.

Beat the margarine until light, then beat in the bananas, a little at a time, and the vanilla essence. Add a little flour with each addition to prevent the mixture from curdling. Mix the remaining flour with the fine oatmeal, baking powder, salt and nuts, and alternately with the date 'sugar' mixture, then fold it into the banana mixture.

Transfer the mixture to a greased 17.5cm/7 inch square baking tin, and level the surface. Sprinkle with the pinhead oatmeal. Bake in a moderate oven, 180°C/350°F/Gas 4, for 1 hour until browned. Cool slightly in the tin, then turn out on to a wire rack to become cold.

OAT BREAD

MAKES TWO 450g/1 lb LOAVES

225g/8 oz medium oatmeal **plus** extra for dusting
1 × 15ml spoon/1 tablespoon oatbran and oatgerm
300ml/½ pint skimmed milk **plus** extra for brushing
25g/1 oz fresh yeast **or** 1 × 15ml spoon/1 tablespoon dried yeast
3 × 15ml spoons/3 tablespoons tepid water
1 × 5ml spoon/1 teaspoon caster sugar
350g/12 oz wholewheat flour
salt
2 × 15ml spoons/2 tablespoons sunflower oil

Soak the oatmeal and oatbran in the milk for at least 30 minutes. Blend the fresh yeast with the water, or reconstitute the dried yeast with the sugar and water. Leave in a warm place for about 20 minutes until frothy.

Stir the flour, salt and oil into the soaked oatmeal. Pour on the yeast liquid, and mix to form a stiff dough.

Dust your hands and a working surface with oatmeal. Knead the dough until smooth, then shape it into a round, and place in an oiled bowl. Cover with oiled polythene, and leave in a warm place for 1-1½ hours until the dough has doubled in size. Turn out the dough, and knead again for about 2 minutes. Divide it into two equal pieces. Place in two greased and floured 450g/1 lb loaf tins, pressing the dough into the corners. Cover with oiled polythene, and leave in a warm place until the dough rises above the tops of the tins.

Brush the tops with milk, and sprinkle with oatmeal. Bake the loaves in a very hot oven, 230°C/450°F/Gas 8, for 30 minutes until they sound hollow when tapped underneath. Cool slightly in the tins, then turn out on to a wire rack to become cold.

Variations

OAT PLAIT
Divide each of the two pieces of risen dough into three. Shape each piece into a long roll or sausage. Take three of the strips, pinch the ends together, and plait the strips loosely. Pinch the other ends together. Repeat with the other three strips, place on an oiled baking sheet, cover with oiled polythene, and leave to prove for a second time until doubled in size. Brush the tops with milk, sprinkle with oatmeal, and bake as above on a greased and floured baking sheet. Cool on a wire rack.

OAT ROLLS
Divide the risen dough into about 18 pieces. Shape into rounds, then leave to prove as for the Oat Plait until doubled in size. Brush the tops with milk, sprinkle with oatmeal, and bake as above for about 20 minutes until the rolls are well risen and sound hollow when tapped. Cool on a wire rack.

CHEESE AND HERB SODA BREAD

MAKES ONE 20cm/8 inch ROUND

350g/12 oz wholewheat self-raising flour
100g/4 oz fine oatmeal **plus** extra for dusting
1 × 5ml spoon/1 teaspoon bicarbonate of soda
salt
25g/1 oz sunflower margarine
2 stalks tender celery, finely chopped
1 small onion, finely chopped

1 × 15ml spoon/1 tablespoon chopped parsley **or** 1 × 5ml spoon/1 teaspoon dried herb
300ml/½ pint buttermilk
milk for brushing
50g/2 oz Edam cheese, grated
2 × 15ml spoons/2 tablespoons rolled porridge oats **or** jumbo oats

Mix together the flour, oatmeal, soda and salt, then rub in the margarine. Stir in the celery, onion and herb, then pour on the buttermilk, and mix quickly to form a firm dough.

Dust your hands and a working surface with oatmeal, and knead the dough until smooth. Shape it into a 20cm/8 inch round, and place on a baking tray sprinkled with oatmeal. Score the top into eight segments, and brush with milk. Mix together the cheese and oats, and press on to the round. Bake in a fairly hot oven, 200°C/400°F/Gas 6, for 35 minutes until well risen and browned. The bread should sound hollow when tapped underneath. Cool on a wire rack. Serve on the day of baking.

Note This bread is especially good with both soups and cheese.

POTATO BREAD

MAKES ONE 450g/1 lb LOAF

175g/6 oz wholewheat flour
50g/2 oz rolled porridge oats **or** jumbo oats
2 × 5ml spoons/2 teaspoons baking powder
salt
1 × 5ml spoon/1 teaspoon paprika

100g/4 oz cooked mashed potato
1 × 15ml spoon/1 tablespoon sunflower oil
200ml/7 fl oz water
2 × 15ml spoons/2 tablespoons medium oatmeal

Mix together the flour, oats, baking powder, salt and paprika, then beat in the mashed potato. Beat in the oil and water, then turn into a 450g/1 lb loaf tin. Sprinkle the oatmeal evenly over the top, then stand the tin on a baking sheet, and bake in a very hot oven, 230°C/450°F/Gas 8, for 25 minutes until well risen and browned. Cool in the tin, then turn out on to a wire rack to become cold.

Note This moist, spicy bread is good with a salad meal.

DATE SANDWICH CAKE

MAKES ONE 22.5cm/9 inch CAKE

50g/2 oz date 'sugar' (page 89)
2 × 15ml spoons/2 tablespoons orange juice
175g/6 oz wholewheat flour
salt
75g/3 oz sunflower margarine
100g/4 oz medium oatmeal
1 × 5ml spoon/1 teaspoon grated orange rind

FILLING

350g/12 oz stoned dried dates, finely chopped
2 × 15ml spoons/2 tablespoons orange juice

Soak the date 'sugar' in the orange juice for at least 10 minutes.

Meanwhile, prepare the filling. Mash the chopped dates with the orange juice, and put to one side.

Mix together the flour and salt. Beat the margarine until it is light, then beat in the date 'sugar', and continue beating until the mixture is creamy. Gradually add the flour, oatmeal and orange rind, and mix with a fork until the mixture resembles coarse crumbs.

Spread half the mixture over the base of a greased 22.5cm/9 inch loose-bottomed cake tin, and press down well with the back of a spoon. Spread with the filling, and cover with the remaining crumb mixture. Bake in a moderate oven, 180°C/350°F/Gas 4, for 45 minutes until well risen. Cool slightly in the tin, then turn out. Serve warm, if possible.

Note Serve with low-fat soured cream or yoghurt as a dessert, or with coffee.

DATE MUFFINS

MAKES 16

50g/2 oz date 'sugar' (page 89)
150ml/¼ pint low-fat yoghurt
100g/4 oz wholewheat self-raising flour
1 × 5ml spoon/1 teaspoon baking powder
salt

1 × 2.5ml spoon/½ teaspoon ground cinnamon
75g/3 oz medium oatmeal
50g/2 oz stoned dried dates, chopped
15g/½ oz sunflower margarine, melted

Stir the date 'sugar' into the yoghurt, then put to one side for at least 10 minutes.

Mix together the flour, baking powder, salt, cinnamon, oatmeal and chopped dates. Stir the melted margarine into the yoghurt and date 'sugar' mixture, and pour this on to the dry ingredients, beating until smooth.

Spoon the mixture into 16 greased patty tins or muffin pans, and bake in a fairly hot oven, 200°C/400°F/Gas 6, for 15-20 minutes until well risen and light. Serve warm if possible, or cold on the day of baking.

APPLE SCONES

MAKES 10

350g/12 oz cooking apples, peeled, cored and chopped
1 × 15ml spoon/1 tablespoon date 'sugar' (page 89)
2 × 15ml spoons/2 tablespoons orange juice
175g/6 oz wholewheat self-raising flour
50g/2 oz medium oatmeal **plus** extra for dusting
salt
1 × 2.5ml spoon/½ teaspoon ground ginger

1 × 2.5ml spoon/½ teaspoon ground cinnamon
40g/1½ oz sunflower margarine
skimmed milk

TOPPING

2 × 15ml spoons/2 tablespoons rolled porridge oats
1 × 2.5ml spoon/½ teaspoon ground cinnamon

Cook the apples with the date 'sugar' and orange juice until they are soft, then beat to a smooth purée. Leave to cool.

Mix together the flour, oatmeal, salt and spices, then rub in the margarine. Add the date 'sugar' purée, then pour on just enough of the milk to make a firm dough.

Dust your hands and a working surface with oatmeal. Knead the dough until smooth. Roll it to a thickness of 2cm/¾ inch, then cut into circles with a 5cm/2 inch round cutter. Re-roll the trimmings and cut out more circles.

Place the dough rounds on a baking tray sprinkled with oatmeal. Brush the tops with milk, and sprinkle with the rolled oats mixed with the cinnamon. Bake in a very hot oven, 230°C/450°F/Gas 8, for 15-20 minutes until well risen and golden-brown. Cool on a wire rack.

Note These scones are delicious spread with more apple purée.

GRIDDLE CAKES

MAKES 12

225g/8 oz wholewheat self-raising flour
100g/4 oz fine oatmeal **plus** extra for dusting
1 × 5ml spoon/1 teaspoon cream of tartar
salt

25g/1 oz sunflower margarine
75g/3 oz currants
300ml/½ pint low-fat yoghurt
150ml/¼ pint buttermilk (approx)
oil for greasing

Mix together the flour, oatmeal, cream of tartar and salt, then rub in the margarine. Stir in the currants, then beat in the yoghurt and just enough of the buttermilk to form a soft dough.

Dust your hands and a working surface with oatmeal. Knead the dough until smooth, then shape it into two rounds each 1.25cm/½ inch thick. Cut each one into six wedges.

Cook the cakes in batches for 4-5 minutes on a hot, lightly greased griddle or in a heavy frying pan until golden-brown on each side. Partly cool on a wire rack, and serve warm, if possible, or cold on the day of baking.

Index